Sermons from the Heart

Steve Starzer

&

Parson's Porch Books

www.parsonsporchbooks.com

Sermons from the Heart

ISBN: Softcover 978-1-951472-31-3

Sermons from the Heart

Contents

Acknowledgements

Where do I begin with my acknowledgements of gratitude? It would really take a full volume to say thank you to everyone who has been so supportive to me not only in compiling this volume but in enabling my ministry for these 40 years. I need to start by thanking God for the gift of my parents, The Rev. Charles F. J. and Elaine K. Starzer. Mom and Dad gave all four of us children a solid home where we were introduced to Jesus Christ and his Church in a loving way. Dad served two congregations during his ministry: the Roseto Presbyterian Church and the First Presbyterian Church of Carbondale both in Pennsylvania. He was a shining example of one who was a Pastor/Preacher. I wish I had had more time to learn more from him. I was blessed to marry the daughter of a colleague, The Rev. John H. Dabback who still stands for me as a wonderful example of what it means to be a Christian Pastor. And my Mother-in-law, Margaret Robb Dabback was a shining example of the Christian faith and is dearly missed.

I have to give credit to the congregations who have allowed me the honor to be called their Pastor. In truth, I learned more from them than they did from me. I am especially grateful to the Wyalusing and Sugar Run Presbyterian Churches for trusting a 25-year-old fresh from the Seminary. Their nurture and love shaped my ministry. The Conklin Presbyterian Church taught me the value of strong relationships and hard work. We grew together over those 20 great years. Fairfield Presbyterian Church has given me the chance to find joy in the final stage of my active ministry. Not everyone has the opportunity to find such a gifted and loving church to lead and I am deeply grateful for the honor and privilege.

I need to thank the men and women of the two Fire Departments where I have been privileged to serve. The Wyalusing Valley Volunteer Fire Department allowed me the chance to do something good and important and to enjoy camaraderie with some great people. Hanover Fire/EMS has allowed me the opportunity to not only rub shoulders with some great people but also challenged me to return to an aspect of ministry that I greatly missed. Both departments helped me to grow as a person and kept me grounded.

Of course the people for whom I am most grateful and to whom I owe the most thanks are my family. My wife Debby brings joy into my life every day. I wouldn't have made it through all these years of ministry without her love and support. My daughter Courtney is a very bright spot in my life. Her vibrancy, her intelligence and her accomplishments encourage me in so many ways. Her husband, Miheer, has been an added blessing to our family for whom I am very grateful. My son, John Charles, (named after his two preacher Grandfathers) is better known to all of us as Chad. His creativity, energy and the amount he has accomplished in his young life inspires me to be a better person. I love each one a little more than the other and that love grows with every passing day.

Foreword

It is both a great honor and a sincere pleasure to introduce to you the Reverend Doctor Stephen Starzer and "Sermons from the Heart. "I have known Steve for nearly a decade now and he is a dear friend of mine. Steve cheerfully loves and is devoted to those he has been called to serve, both in the church and community where he serves as pastor, and the many area firefighters and emergency services personnel to whom he ministers as chaplain. I am certain the sermons on the following pages will clearly communicate Steve's love for God, family and flock.

"Sermons from the Heart" is quite an appropriate title for this book. Steve approaches all he does with a kind and caring nature that is rare to find but a joy to behold. This caring nature shines through in his preaching style. Though educational and steeped in the Reformed tradition, his sermons tend to be less like a lecture and more like a friend sharing a story. Frequently, the heart is not only the source of the message, but also the target.

Steve is also a lover of stories. Often you will find him either intently listening as someone shares a tale with him or heartily sharing a story of his own. The stories he has to share from his childhood, from his nearly four decades of ministry, and even from his father-- who was also a Presbyterian pastor-- are plentiful and always seem to be apt. In the following pages, you will find stories not just interwoven into the sermons, but also stories detailing the circumstances during which the sermons were given. The drama of the story is what helps communicate the message and make it memorable.

There are innumerable scientific studies that show our human brains are better able to retain information when a story is involved. Even the Scriptures utilize stories and drama to communicate God's Word to us. The ram that gets caught in the thicket for Abraham to use as a sacrifice is a good story about God providing, but only slightly memorable in and of itself. Adding the events leading up to that moment--Abraham believing that he would need to sacrifice his son Isaac-- makes God's provision more meaningful and the story more memorable. Include the details of Isaac being the only son of

Abraham and his wife Sarah, that Isaac was a gift from God to the barren elderly couple, and that Isaac would be the one with whom God would establish his covenant, and the meaning in the story grows deeper and richer.

The parables of Jesus are also stories to help our understanding of God's will for us. Frequently, we find a new or deeper meaning in the parables when we learn either to whom Jesus is addressing the story or the events that immediately preceded it. The drama leading up to the parable can be as important as the parable itself in understanding God's message for us. I believe that is what you will find to be true in these sermons. The circumstances surrounding the sermon give added meaning to the message being conveyed.

So I invite you to grab a hot cup of tea or coffee, sit back and turn the page as a loving pastor and lover of stories shares with you some of the most meaningful sermons of his career - sermons from his heart to yours.

J. R. Marker, III
Elder
Fairfield Presbyterian Church

Preface

H.H. Farmer was quoted as saying that the sermon is the word of God through the personality of the preacher. I think that is absolutely true. The preacher is without cause to speak without the pages of Holy Scripture. The pages of the Bible are brought home when they are communicated through our own lives and experiences. I know that in my own situation, my preaching ministry is shaped by my own life and by the shared experiences I have had with the congregations I have been blessed to serve over the past 38 plus years.

Of course my preaching ministry started out under the leadership and nurture of my own Dad, The Rev. Charles F. J. Starzer, who was the ultimate Pastor/Preacher. He deeply loved the congregations he served over the course of his 44 years of ordained ministry. But he knew that being a Pastor/Preacher was probably the hardest job that one could imagine. He never encouraged me to follow in his footsteps and he gave me every opportunity to say that I wasn't called to it. In retrospect the opportunities he gave me early on to preach may very well have been designed to make me stop and think before getting in too deep! The first sermons I ever preached were in the summer before I started college. I spent two Sundays preaching to the congregation which gathered in the "chapel" of Fairview State Hospital for the Criminally Insane in Waymart Pennsylvania.

Imagine my anxiety walking down hard tile corridors hearing the huge oak doors closing behind me with the loud clank of the brass locks sealing me in. Escorted by hospital personnel to the auditorium there to find myself at the makeshift pulpit staring out at a couple hundred residents and about 20 attendants assigned for my security. I left that day exhausted by the experience when it dawned on me that I had one more Sunday my Dad committed me to preach there!

The second place I preached that summer was a few Sundays at the Forest City, PA Presbyterian Church. Relieved to know that I would no longer need escorts or security, I was nonetheless overwhelmed by the fact that this tiny congregation had already voted to close, and

I was just filling a need until the final service was held. At least they couldn't say I killed the church!

Asking my Dad sometime later why he got me those opportunities he said, "If you can preach in those circumstances, you can preach anywhere." He knew that being a Preacher/Pastor was more than just reading some theological/Biblical paper for those who were gathered. He knew that every setting was different. He knew that the people to whom we would preach had different fears and hopes. We had to understand that before we could share God's Word with them.

Personality is a part of preaching. The personality of the hearers and the personality of the speaker. God's word to God's people is not a dry exercise in knowledge imparted from one to another. It is the very Love of God shared with a people who desperately need that love through the words of one who equally needs that love and is compelled to share that love.

So it is, in that light, that I offer you these sermons. I am no master pulpiteer. I am instead simply one who has experienced the love of God in Jesus Christ through the Holy Spirit and wants to share that love. I am nothing more than that.

Introduction

Why do I call this volume "Sermons from the Heart"? It actually has two meanings for me. It is a description of my style of preaching. I do not preach from a text and rarely from notes. I don't technically memorize my sermon but instead I know it by heart when I step into the pulpit. It's not the easiest way but for me it is the only way because I want my preaching to be a conversation between myself and the people I love and serve. So it is that I find the second reason I entitled this book "Sermons from the Heart." Every time I preach, I am preaching as one who wants to share what is on my heart to people who are in my heart.

Each of the sermons included in this volume plays a role in giving a glimpse of my preaching ministry. These sermons are not handpicked because they are the best sermons I ever preached. I wouldn't know how to judge which ones those might be. Instead they are simply chosen to represent the work I have done over these nearly four decades as a Pastor/Preacher. I have chosen sermons from each of the three phases of my ordained ministry. A few date back to my youthful days joyfully serving the Wyalusing and Sugar Run Presbyterian Churches in Pennsylvania, more come from my twenty years given lovingly to the people of Conklin Presbyterian Church in New York and a few more are from my present ministry among the wonderful people of Fairfield Presbyterian Church in Mechanicsville, Virginia.

Many books of sermons are organized in a manner that is useful to the preacher who enjoys reading them to sharpen their own skills or for their own spiritual growth. Many I have read are organized according to the Christian calendar and others are gathered under one overarching topic. This volume is going to be a little different. In the Fire Service we have a catch phrase that helps to guide us: situational awareness. This humble book of sermons is organized into categories which reflect the situations in which I found myself as Pastor/Preacher. I think this is what Karl Barth truly meant when he said that we should preach with the Bible in one hand and the newspaper in the other. I don't think it was so much a call to be overly prophetic or to use the headlines to guide our preaching, but

I believe it was for us to be aware of where our people's hearts and minds would be. I also believe it was a reminder to know where our own hearts were as well.

Unlike most volumes of sermons, this one includes some very personal sermons, one's written when my children were born, and ones written when I had to say goodbye to those whom I loved dearly and deeply. I have also included with the permission of the families a funeral sermon and a wedding sermon. Preaching is not a Sunday morning only responsibility.

How do I imagine these sermons to be used? My hope and prayer is that God will somehow use these to edify and bless the reader. I wish I had a volume like this available to my students when I was involved in the lay preachers' programs in both Lackawanna and Susquehanna Valley Presbyteries. I would hope that a student learning the art of preaching could gain some insight from the journey upon which these sermons will take them. I pray too that these sermons will be a reminder to the churches whom I served that I loved them deeply and wanted nothing more than to help them to know Jesus Christ and experience His Kingdom. In all situations, if there is any good which arises from these pages, to God be all the glory and honor.

Gifts of Love: The Greatest Commandment

Mark 12: 28-34

November 6, 2018

During this past church year Darren and I have been trying, on a regular basis, to help us to see and understand the meaning and the purpose of the church year. In the early days of the church year we talked with you about the fact that it was designed by the early church to help somebody who was new to the faith get a full and complete understanding of what the Christian faith is all about. And it was lined out and marked out by all those wonderful seasons and holidays that would we enjoy so much: Advent leading into Christmas, Lent leading into Easter, Easter leading into Pentecost, and so on. We wanted you to see that it gives us a form upon which we can hang our understanding of what it means to be followers of Jesus Christ.

Now the church year does not follow the calendar year, because November is the end of the church year and Advent, starting in December, is the beginning of the next church year. Obviously, we begin with the incarnation of Jesus – his birth as the babe of Bethlehem. That is the beginning, so that you can have that in your mind. But this is the end of the church year and as such, as you end anything, you try to wrap things up. This season has historically been called the season of Pentecost or the extended season of Pentecost. But it also has another name. It's called Ordinary Time which I think is the better name for it because Ordinary Time is where we live. We live in an ordinary world with ordinary days and a certain ordinariness to our lives. We get up in the morning, we have breakfast, start our day's activities, have some lunch and afternoon activities, dinner and so on and start it all over again the next day. So we live, all of us, I think it's safe to say, rather ordinary lives. Therefore to understand the Gospel of Jesus Christ for those ordinary days this time is essential for us.

15

And historically the Christian church has chosen to set aside the month of November not by decree but just by practice and habit to be a season of Thanksgiving and to allow us to ponder how it is, in light of all that we have seen and learned about who Jesus Christ is and what he has done for us, to learn how to live with it in ordinary days.

Now I want us to look at a familiar passage. I know you have heard it a hundred thousand times before but let's listen to it again. It's found in the Gospel according to Mark in the twelfth chapter. It's a wonderful story out of Jesus' life and ministry. The twelfth chapter beginning with the 28th verse:

"One of the scribes came near and heard them disputing with one another and seeing that Jesus answered them well he asked him, 'Which commandment is first of all?' Jesus answered 'the first is hear O' Israel the Lord our God, the Lord is one. You shall love the Lord your God with all your heart, with all your soul, with all your mind and with all your strength. The second is this – You shall love the neighbor as yourself. There is no other commandment greater than these.' Then the scribe said to Jesus, 'You're right teacher, you have truly said that he is one and beside him there is no other and to love him with all the heart, with all the understanding, with all the strength and to love one's neighbor as one's self. This is much more important than all whole burnt offerings and sacrifices. When Jesus saw that he had answered wisely, he said to the scribe, 'You are not far from the kingdom of God.' After that no one dared to ask him any questions."

May the Lord bless this a portion from his holy word.

It is a familiar passage is it not? If I had walked up to any of you this morning and said, "what is the greatest commandment?" you would have said "ooh ooh I've got that one! I know what it is, I remember that story. It's the story where Jesus said that the greatest commandment is to love the Lord your God with your heart, mind, soul and your strength and then he said to love your neighbor as yourself as a very close second." Familiar isn't it? How many times have you heard a sermon or a Sunday School lesson on this topic and learned that this is the core and the essence of what it means to respond to the good news of Jesus Christ. How is it that we ought to live our lives in light of that Gospel story? In light of all we have learned through the Christian year and as we're drawing it to a conclusion, what is it that is the take-away for us? What is it that we need to have as a part of our lives in our ordinary living? To love the Lord your God with heart, mind, soul and strength. And to love your neighbor as yourself.

There's a good chance right now you're all sitting out there going "that's all well and good Steve. Tell me something I don't know." There's a phrase, a saying, "familiarity brings blindness." Sometimes you can know something so well that you don't see it clearly. And there's a few things in this that maybe we miss because we know the answers so readily, we're ready to take the test, you can do fill in the blank, you can do matching, you can do essay and think I'm going to get this one right because I know the answer to it. But you might miss some very important parts to this puzzle. You see there are some very interesting pieces in here that maybe our familiarity with this story blinds us from seeing them. I mean, did you notice that the teacher, the scribe, the lawyer said, "Teacher what is the greatest commandment?" He asked in the singular. And Jesus answered in the plural.

The lawyer wanted to get the answer from Jesus in terms of what is the one thing I have to do to be a part of the kingdom of God. And Jesus comes back with not one but two. You see Jesus recognizes the fact that to love the Lord your God with your heart, your mind, your soul and strength inevitably, inevitably, means that you must love your neighbor as yourself. You cannot love the Lord your God with heart, mind, soul and strength and ignore your neighbor in need. It cannot be done. I mean, wasn't it Jesus who said, "if you've done it unto the least of these you've done it unto me?" You see to love the Lord your God absolutely means that we love our neighbors as ourselves. Because one of the most important ways we show our love for God is by showing that love to those whom he has placed into our lives. You can't separate those two commandments.

The scribe, maybe he was looking for a loophole, maybe he was searching for the easy way or maybe he was wanting something that would make his life simpler. Don't we all want something to make our lives simpler? But Jesus didn't give that to him. He said if you love the Lord your God that means you're going to love your neighbor. It's as easy as that and as difficult as that.

Something else you might have missed. You know when it was all said and done the scribe, the teacher, commends Jesus for his wisdom, thanks him for his wisdom and Jesus responds by saying, "you're very close to the kingdom of God." Close but no cigar. You're not quite there. What did Jesus see that told him that the scribe wasn't quite there yet. Did you listen? When Jesus answered the scribe, he said "you must love the Lord your God with your heart, your mind, your soul, your strength." When the scribe responded back to him and said, "thank you Lord, I appreciate your wisdom. I do know that I must love the Lord my God with my heart, my mind, my strength." He didn't say anything about his soul.

He dropped his soul from the answer. Now, let's not be mistaken because our minds always go to the Greek philosophers and their understanding of soul and the soul is a spiritual part of us. It has nothing to do with the physical part of us. And you know the Greek philosophers talked about the soul being freed from the body and all this sort of stuff but that's not what Jesus, that's not the Jewish way of thinking that's not the Hebrew way of thinking. When they understood soul, it wasn't something that was separate. They understood when they spoke of the soul, they understood it as the core of who a person is. A part of who a person is, the central guide for their identification, was the soul of the man or the woman. Jesus didn't want just the outward actions of love. As important and as good as those are, he didn't want them to think we can love the Lord our God with our heart and our mind and our strength but not with who we are. You see, Jesus knew that if he asked that scribe who are you? Tell me about who you are, the scribe would say well I am a teacher of the law. I studied under this person and that person and

I have served here, and I have served there. He would share his identity from a self-perspective. We do that. I mean, you ask most any man, tell me about yourself, and they will say, "well, my career was this, I worked for 30 years here and 10 years there and I did this in my career and I did that in my career and I identify as a carpenter, a lawyer, a doctor, or a teacher or something else." A woman will generally speak, now these are generalities – please don't catch me on these, but a woman will generally speak of family. You know I am the wife of such and such and the mother of these kids and I have grandkids and I have great grandkids. They identify themselves that way. But Jesus is saying that's all well and good, those are wonderful. But who is the soul of who you are? Where is your identity? You see in this what Jesus wants us to say, if somebody asks us "who are you?"

If you love the Lord your God with your heart, your mind and your soul and your strength, then your answer is going to be, "I am a follower of Jesus Christ. That is the core of my identity. That is the core of who I am." We see that the scribe very well may not have been ready to find his whole identity in his relationship with God. He's willing to do what it took to show God's love with his mind, his intellect, his heart, his emotions, his strength, his energy but he wasn't quite ready to find his persona, his identity, his soul in being a follower of God's rule and God's love. It's a familiar passage. A story told over and over and over again and its beauty of simplicity of taking the core of all of the laws and rules and commandments of the Old Testament and boiling them down to these two commandments seems simple. But to love the Lord our God with heart, mind, soul and strength is not so simple at all. Will you pray with me?

Almighty God, giver of all life, giver of all love. We do seek to be your followers, to find our purpose, our identity, ourselves in the acknowledgement that Jesus Christ is Lord of our lives. Help us O Lord to love our neighbors as ourselves as we seek to love you with our hearts, our minds, our strength, and yes, even our identities. We pray this is Jesus' name. Amen.

The Upside-Down Kingdom Where the Blind Can See

Mark 10: 46-52

October 28, 2018

You know we come to worship today with our hearts broken by the news. None of us can begin to understand why such a terrible tragedy, travesty could occur. And if you've ever been to Pittsburgh, the Squirrel Hill section is a beautiful neighborhood. It's just one of those little communities within the city that is very appealing, and you can tell that it's a close-knit well-maintained community. It's hard for us to begin to understand how someone, how anyone, could be at a point where they would do such violence to a group of people for no other reason than their heritage, their faith, their desire to worship together within that faith. It's beyond our comprehension how such hatred could ever exist in this world. But it does. It is the ugly truth that there is anti-Semitism that exists in this world. And that never should be, that never ever should be. And I have to blame the church in some ways. Maybe it's because our silence over the years, maybe we have not said loudly and clearly enough that there is no room for anti-Semitism within the Christian faith. We have not said loudly and clearly enough that to be anti-Semitic is to be anti-Christian because we as Christians are grafted on to the root of Jesse. The Jewish faith is our heritage. The people killed in Pittsburgh are our extended family. We read the Hebrew Scriptures and we see in there God's working in the world. We see in there the foretelling of a Messiah. We see in the Hebrew Scriptures that we share with the Jewish people the words that lead us to see and understand the grace of God that we have seen so clearly in the person and work of Jesus Christ. To be anti-Semitic is to be anti-Christian and a very real sense to be anti-Jesus Christ himself. For the Lord and Savior that we worship, that we seek to serve is Jewish. I do not understand or begin to even comprehend in any small way how anyone could hate a people for their faith, especially when it is a faith that we share with them. But it's easy to just put people into categories or put people into pigeonholes and cease to see them as people. To see them only as a category; to see them only as a type that we see them to be. Jesus saw that in his day. He saw that people would stereotype others and place them into categories and to cast them to the side as unworthy or as of less value than others. He saw that people often looked at others and did not see people.

This series of sermons that we are doing helps us to see how Jesus took common perceptions and flipped them upside down or turn them all the way around. And we look today at a passage of scripture from the Gospel according to Mark, the tenth chapter. A passage that is probably extremely familiar to all of us – the healing of blind Bartimaeus. Rings a bell, doesn't it? A familiar story, one that we have heard in our Sunday School classes, one that we have probably heard in sermons in the past and we look at this story and we see it as one that we place into a category. We place it into the category of understanding Jesus in light of generally two categories: his teachings and his miracles. And so we look at this and we see Jesus healing blind Bartimaeus and just put it up into that category. Just one more proof, one more example in the person and work of Jesus Christ of his miraculous nature, of his divinity, of his exceptionalism of setting Jesus above.

But let's read this passage carefully. Let's hear what's really going on here. And let's seek to understand how Jesus was turning things upside down in his day. In the tenth chapter of Mark beginning with the 46th verse:

> "They came to Jericho. As he and his disciples and a large crowd were leaving Jericho, Bartimaeus son of Timaeus, a blind beggar was sitting by the roadside.
>
> When he heard that it was Jesus of Nazareth, he began to shout out and say, 'Jesus, Son of David, have mercy on me!' Many sternly ordered him to be quiet, but he cried out even more loudly, 'Son of David, have mercy on me!' Jesus stood still and said, 'Call him here.' And they called the blind man, saying to him,
>
> 'Take heart; get up he's calling you.' So throwing off his cloak, he sprang up and came to Jesus. Then Jesus said to him, 'What do you want me to do for you?'

The blind man said to him, 'My teacher, let me see again.' Jesus said to him, 'Go, your faith has made you well.' Immediately he regained his sight and followed Jesus on the way."

May the Lord bless this a portion from his holy word.

It is a wonderful story. It's a heart-warming story is it not? It is one of those miraculous stories that we love to hear. Stories that show Jesus' compassion, stories that show Jesus' strength and ability, stories the show how Jesus takes somebody and makes them whole. He takes this blind man and helps him to see. It's a heartwarming story: a story that we can look at it ourselves and we are happy for Bartimaeus; that this man who went from darkness to light, that he saw things that you and I take for granted because we have our sight, we can see things, we can appreciate the beauty of a pink rose coming to bloom. We can appreciate the beauty of the blue in the sky contrasted by the puffy white clouds. We can appreciate that everybody's face is a little bit different and we can see those distinctions from each other and recognize friends, recognize family, recognize others and we are glad to greet them and for Bartimaeus this was something new and different for him and we are glad for him in what he experienced. We are glad for him in the sight that he gained.

But if we look at this story, if we look at this incident out of Jesus' life and all we see is a heartwarming story of Jesus giving sight to someone who could not see, then we're missing half the story that happened here. We're missing an important piece of this story that I'm sure Jesus wants us to see and to hear. Did you notice what was happening on the side of the road? Bartimaeus somehow or another, as Vicky told us in the children's message, the blind develops other abilities to see things that we don't have. Bartimaeus somehow or another, maybe it was the rush of the crowd, maybe it was all the noise, maybe it was people bumping into him. Who knows what it was, but he realized something big was happening and something was going on there? And somebody was kind enough to tell him that the crowd that was gathering were people who wanted to see Jesus of Nazareth as he came along that road. Now this, we're led to believe, was Bartimaeus' corner. This was the one that he sat at and begged to get his subsistence so that he could live. There was no safety net for those who couldn't earn a living, there were no social programs, and there was nothing for them other than the generosity of those who might throw a coin into their cup as they begged along the side of the road. But Bartimaeus knew that this was somebody special who was coming, and he began to cry out, "Jesus, son of David, have mercy on me!" He was trying to get Jesus' attention and was probably shouting at the top of his lungs because he couldn't see where Jesus was. He had to rely upon the sound, and he had to rely upon his own voice calling out loud enough for Jesus to hear him and to notice him. And so Bartimaeus was doing exactly what any of us would do in that same situation. He was crying out for help from Jesus.

But those who were around him said "Shut-up blind man. Pipe down. You're not the type of person that Jesus should have to deal with." You see, in that society, in that time, if you had something wrong with you, whatever it might be, it was your fault. If you were blind or if you were lame or if you had leprosy or whatever it might be, you were deemed unworthy. You had whatever you had because of something you had done or something your father before you had done you had no right to complain because you got what you deserved. So they would look at these blind people, look at these lame people, they would look at all these people with all these afflictions and infirmities and they would put them into this category over here and see them not as people but see them as something less, something other, something unworthy. As a matter of fact, even Bartimaeus' name calls to question how he was perceived because Timaeus is not a Jewish name. Some scholars believe that Timaeus means worthless. That he is Bartimaeus, son of worthlessness. No wonder they were trying to get him to shut-up. "You're worthless, you have no voice here." But Jesus, the one who turns the world upside-down saw in Bartimaeus, not one who was worthless but saw in him somebody worth being loved. He took him out of that nameless category and brought him to the center of attention. And Jesus said, "Send him my way; I want to talk to him." And Bartimaeus somehow or another made his way through the crowd and got to be face to face with Jesus and Jesus said, "What is it I can do for you son?" And Bartimaeus said simply, "I want to be able to see" and Jesus healed his sight. And suddenly the darkness was gone; suddenly he could see.

Jesus calls us to not see people as categories. To not place values on people but to see people in the same way that Jesus did. That every single person is loveable in God's eyes and for us to see that loveableness, even when it might not be readily apparent to us. Jesus saw in Bartimaeus somebody worth loving. Not as somebody who got what he deserved, somebody who was worthless, somebody who was just as well left by the side of the road but saw him as somebody who was worthy to be loved. We still have a little bit of a hard time with that. We still look at people and we have this almost innate desire to categorize them for their value, for their worth. I just got a letter, about a six-page handwritten letter. Do you believe that? A handwritten letter six pages long! It's sitting on my desk if you don't believe me. It's from a young man who was a member of the church in Conklin and I remember him as a youth, a little boy. He didn't have much. He came to church with his grandmother because his home life was centered in his grandparent's home and he didn't have, well, he didn't have an average ability intellectually. He was probably deemed by the system as below average, maybe even well below average in his intellectual abilities. His social skills – not everyone recognized his awkwardness as endearing. If you looked at him, talked with him, you might be led by society's standards to declare that he had nothing to commend him to us. But he's now 30-31, and in this letter that he wrote, he shares that he is in a hard time right now. He is going through a very difficult period in his life. He is working through some issues that he has to work through. But this letter, this six-page letter talks about how the church has loved him and how the church is still loving and supporting him. Somebody that society says has little or no value, found in the body of Christ, a place to be loved. Not for what he does, not for what he can give, not for who he is related to, but simply because they see in him the same thing that Jesus sees in him. Here is somebody that, if there was nobody else on this earth, if there was just this one man, that Jesus would have been willing to die upon the cross for him.

Jesus turns the world upside down. He calls us to love those whom we see as unlovable. He calls us to love those whom we consider our enemies. He calls us to see in each person what God sees – somebody who is worth loving. Yes, anti-Semitism is anti-Christian. There should never ever, never be any violence against anyone for any persons, especially because they are something different than what we are. We're called to love and to see in each person how God loves them and to share that love with everyone. Would you pray with me?

Oh God of love and God of mercy, it's so much easier for us if you would let us put people into categories so we could know whom to deal with and whom we can just ignore. But you haven't called us to do what is easy. You've called us to do what is right. Help us, O Lord, to not be so blind that we cannot see in others what you see as so loveable in them. Help us to be your bearers of that love in a world that so desperately needs it. We pray this in Jesus' name and for his sake. Amen.

We Had Hoped

Luke 24: 13-32

September 23, 2007

Installation of The Rev. Joe Hein, a former staff member of the Conklin Presbyterian Church, as Pastor of the Westminster Presbyterian Church in Middletown, N.J.

It was a Sunday afternoon a long time ago in a place far distant from here. Two people were walking in the countryside making their way toward home. It had been one of those weeks when nothing went the way they had hoped, and their faces were etched with the stories of two broken spirits. Another man caught up with them and began to walk side by side with them. This man whom they did not recognize seemed to be untouched by the events of the past week. In fact he asked those whose walk he joined why their faces were so downcast.

They told the one who had joined them the whole story. The story of what was and what might have been. They told a story of one who worked miracles and filled people with hope. They told the story of one who dashed their hopes since he no longer was because he had been crucified and died. "Oh, how we hoped" they moaned, "oh, how we hoped."

Their faces betrayed the fact that they were living in the past. It is easy to get so caught up in the past that we can no longer see the present nor the future. The two men walking along the road that day were so lost in their own despair that they didn't even recognize the man who was walking along side of them. Because they were dwelling in the past, they didn't realize that their very future was right there next to them.

I was privy to a conversation one day between an older couple I knew. The husband was what some people might call "a cranky old man" who wouldn't be pleased by anything. He kept going on and on about how he wished it were the "good ole days". Finally his ever-patient wife had had enough of that talk and she burst into the conversation. "You want the 'good old days'? Did you forget that we had no running water in the house, and it was a long cold walk to that drafty old outhouse? Did you forget that we never had two nickels to rub together so it didn't really matter whether bread was $.12 (cents) a loaf or not because we still couldn't afford it? Did you forget that the only heat in this old house was that wood stove in the kitchen and if you walked two feet away from it you'd half freeze to death? You old coot, these are the good ole days and you don't even know it!"

It is easy to dwell in the past. And there is no greater culprit for that than the Christian Church. There is a wonderful little book entitled, "The Seven Last Words of the Church": we never did it that way before! When I was in Seminary, I was asked to fill the pulpit of a church in the Wyoming Valley of Pennsylvania for a couple of months. The Clerk of Session took me around for a tour of the facilities and not a room went by where she didn't say to me, "Why, I remember when..."

To know and enjoy history is good! We can learn a great deal from remembering the past. But we cannot live in the past because it will never be the way that it was. Time always marches ahead and brings with it many changes. To dwell in the past is to miss today and to lose tomorrow. And to dwell in the past often times obscures our vision so that we cannot see what really is. Joe Garagiola was a mediocre major league baseball player at best. But he loves to tell the story of how, when he retired from professional baseball, he began to tour the country speaking at athletic banquets and other sports gatherings. In the first years that he was speaking he would be introduced as "former major league player, Joe Garagiola". After he had been retired a few years he noticed that more and more often he would be introduced as "former all-star catcher, Joe Garagiola". As time went on the introduction became, "One of the all-time great catchers, Joe Garagiola". Our vision can become easily distorted if we look only toward the past.

Those two people walking along the road were so engulfed in the past that they could not see who it was walking shoulder to shoulder with them. The words of the song from a few years back said, "You don't know what you've got 'til it's gone" and that is just what happened to those two men on the road to Emmaus. They didn't realize who was with them until after he had gone. They could have enjoyed him - they could have asked all of those questions which were burning within their hearts - but they missed the opportunity.

In our Christian lives and in our life together as the Church we often miss Jesus. He promised us that wherever two or more are gathered in his name there he would be in the midst of us. Jesus keeps his promises - but we have to keep our eyes open and our hearts prepared to recognize him when he is walking side by side with us. One of my favorite Christian plaques is the one of "Footprints in the Sand". It tells the story of a walk side by side with Jesus as seen in the two sets of footprints in the sand. The speaker notes that there was a time when there was only one set of impressions in the sand and complains, wanting to know why Jesus wasn't there side by side with him when he needed him most. Jesus points out that the speaker was wrong. The one set of footprints in the sand were not the man's but those of the savior who was carrying the man through those times of struggle.

If we are living today with our eyes wide open and our hearts prepared, we will see that Christ is with us today. Christ is here to touch our lives, to guide and to direct us, to give us comfort and hope and assurance. Christ is here to work miracles in this time and this place. He is here but we need to look for him in those ordinary places. It is there in the commonplace that Christ works his miracles and shows himself to us. It is when we are going what we are supposed to be doing that Christ startles us with his miraculous presence.

When those two people along the road opened their hearts and their home to that stranger along the road a miracle happened. Through the very ordinary sharing of an evening meal their eyes were opened, and their hearts were strangely warmed. When they broke bread together as friends, they saw Jesus. Out of the past they saw the present and the future. In the ordinary they saw the extraordinary.

Our Presbyterian way of doing business seems to have people yearn for a simpler time. Long before computers churches would reach out to Pastors they knew and look for recommendations. A call would be offered. Clean, neat and done! We long for simpler times! We long for the days when Pastors stayed in one place forever. We long for the days when everything was cheaper, including having Pastors. You trudged along with all the work involved with electing a Pastor Nominating Committee. Forms were filled out. Letters were written. Phone calls made. Meetings attended. Interviews being held. Doing all things "decently and in order" - doing the ordinary work of the Church and a miracle happened. Instead of dwelling in the past and moping, "Oh how we hoped" you dwelt in today and your hopes have been fulfilled through a lot of little miracles in the ordinary things.

Miracles? Yes, miracles - how else do you explain a young man who grew up with the hopes and expectations of playing Major League Baseball becoming a wonderful Pastor? Was it merely an ecclesiastical process or just maybe was the Holy Spirit moving in the hearts of a man from Binghamton, NY and a team of people in Middletown, N.J.? And don't you think it is at least a minor miracle that all the pieces of this puzzle came together to make this day a reality. Instead of looking back you continued to do the ordinary and yes mundane and in through that God has brought about something very good here!

God works miracles! Jesus is with us today - let us vow to keep our eyes wide open for his presence among us. Let us continue to do the ordinary as he continues to surprise us with the extraordinary. Amen.

What's in the Bag?

Romans 8: 26-39

June 8, 2014

I have to tell all of you a little story. Amy inspired me. Amy Atkinson's children's messages always inspires me. When I was in the Wyalusing Church, one Easter Sunday, there was a young woman by the name of Kay Homer who came to church with her three young boys all under the age of five. She came in with what looked like the world's largest purse you'd ever seen. She sat in the second row up front so that I would see her and her kids. And all through the service I just kept watching her pull stuff out of that bag, one item after another item after another item, Cheerios, toys for them to play with, wipes to clean them up and everything and I just thought this is the most amazing mother that I had ever seen because her three boys behaved so well in church that day and I knew she had everything in that bag for them. But the kicker was this, this is true now, when the service was all done, I saw her pull out of the bag a Dustbuster and she cleaned up the pew where she was sitting with her boys.

The passage of scripture that we have is part of, what in my mind, may be the greatest chapter ever written. It is as full as that young mother's bag. The eighth chapter of Romans is just so full or truth and wisdom and we're only going to read 14 verses out of it. But it's one of those chapters that if I had the ability to memorize things well, instead of having a memory verse I would have a memory chapter and it would be the eighth chapter of Romans because it is so full of good stuff! Now the problem with it is that, in many people's minds, this portion that I'm going to be reading is one of those portions that has become associated with funerals. This is very often times a passage that families like to have read when they have lost somebody they loved. And that's a good thing. I'm not saying it's a bad thing. That's a good thing but this is really a passage that is an everyday sort of passage. This is a passage of scripture that can guide and direct us in any situation of our lives, in good times and in bad times, in the ups and downs and ins and out of life. This has a great deal of wisdom for all of us to consider. So in the 8th chapter, toward the end, we begin with the 26th verse.

> "In the same way, the Spirit helps us in our weakness. We do not know what we ought to pray, but the Spirit himself intercedes for us with groans that words cannot express. And he who searches our hearts knows the mind of the Spirit, because the Spirit intercedes for the saints in accordance with God's will. And we know that in all things God works for the good of those who love him, who have been called according to his purpose. For those God foreknew he also predestined to be conformed to the likeness of his Son, that he might be the firstborn among many brothers. And those whom he predestined, he also called; those he called, he also justified; those he justified, he also glorified. What, then, shall we say in response to this? If God is for us, who can be against us? He who did not spare his own Son, but gave him up for us all—how will he not also, along with him, graciously give us all things? Who will bring any charge against those whom God has chosen? It is God who justifies. Who is he that condemns? Christ Jesus who died—more than that, who was raised to life—is at the right hand of God and is also interceding for us. Who shall separate us from the love of Christ? Shall trouble or hardship or persecution or famine or nakedness or danger or sword? As it is written: 'For your sake we face death all day long; we are considered as sheep to be slaughtered.' No, in all things we are more than conquerors through him who loved us. For I am convinced that neither death nor life, neither angels nor demons, neither the present nor the future, nor any powers, neither height nor depth, nor anything else in all creation, will be able to separate us from the love of God that is in Christ Jesus our Lord."

May the Lord bless this a portion from his holy word to all of us.

This is a passage which is oftentimes associated with the hard times of our lives, but I do not think it ought to be. I think it ought to be a part of our lives day in and day out. Because in every day of our lives we have decisions that we have to make, we have struggles we go through, we have areas that we deal with in our lives and we need to always remember that God is with us in every situation. In the good and in the bad, he is always present with us. One of the things that I love about this passage is that first section is about praying and how the Holy Spirit is with us because there are so many times in our lives where we're just not quite sure how to pray. And more often than not we think of that in the hard times where we're struggling to find the words but sometimes, we're just even sure how to pay in the good times. I had somebody just a week or so ago ask me the question of whether he can pray for something that might be construed as being selfish. That's a good question, isn't it? Now for most of us our first response would be, "Well you probably ought not to pray for something that's purely selfish, you ought not to pray for something.... I don't buy lottery tickets, but you know, obviously, I don't want to be in a position where I'm praying that my lottery ticket wins. I can tell you right now that's probably not a good prayer.

But there are those times in our life where we're not sure how to pray or we're not sure whether we ought to pray. Those are the times when the Holy Spirit can be with us. Because I think the key that Paul is trying to help us to see is that God is in a constant relationship with us, even when we don't realize it. Even when we're not sure how to pray or what to pray or even when we don't realize that we are praying, the Holy Spirit is still with us and interceding with us and that is so good to know.

So the question is never whether something is an appropriate prayer or not, the question is never whether we ought to pray or not. What the question is comes down to this: since we are in a relationship with God are we understanding that he is present in our lives? Are we allowing the Holy Spirit to guide and direct us in every aspect of our lives? Even when we're not sure whether this is something we ought to be praying for, even asking that question, simply asking that question is a prayer. And the Holy Spirit is making that prayer understandable to God. The Holy Spirit is our communicator, our guide, our translator in prayer. I think that's wonderful precisely because there are so many times in our lives when we just don't know how to pray, therefore, to know that we have the Holy Spirit within us! It is the Holy Spirit who takes our thought process, who takes the churning in our stomach - whatever it might be-and turns it into a conversation with God! God comes into our hearts and into our lives to guide and direct us in any decision, and in every situation.

I have to be honest with you folks, I should never have taken a big chunk of text like this to preach on because there are like 82 sermons in this text that I want to do and so if you're not out of here by 11, you're going to have to go because the 11 o'clock congregation is going to want to be here. It is just so chock full of good stuff in here! It really is like the purse! But the other element of this is one of the misunderstandings of this passage ...this misuse is like fingernails on the chalkboard to me! I have such a hard time when some people take this passage and they think that what it is saying is that God predestined everything to happen. They believe it says that if something happens to us, it because God caused it to happen and more often than not what I hear being said it's in some negative situation, such as when someone is going through a tragedy. I've often thought that someday I'm going to write a book entitled "Things Not to Say in the Funeral Home" You don't know how many times, in a funeral home, I've heard somebody come up and say, "well, you know God has a plan and God did this according to his plan." Tragedy happens. Someone dies in a car accident. A young child drowns. A person dies of cancer and leaves a young family behind. For someone to say that God caused that or to say that God planned that or that it was part of God's plan is missing the point of this passage by 180 degrees! Instead, what this passage is telling us is that God is with us in every situation. In every situation! No matter how dire the situation may be, no matter how difficult the situation may be, no matter how hurtful the situation may be, God is able to bring something good out of it. God is able to redeem that situation. That's what God's plan is. That's what God predestines us for. His will for us is to be redeemed and for some good to come out of even the worst of situations. God doesn't cause the bad situations to happen, but God is present when those situations happen and is working with us to redeem the situation.

And another element of this... this is kind of like my pet peeve day, so I'll get another pet peeve out of the way on you. One of my pet peeves is the phrase "God will never give you more than you can handle." Sorry, my blood pressure is going up right now just thinking about that phrase. First of all, God doesn't give you those difficulties to handle and secondly, whatever the situation is it's not for us to handle alone. We will never find ourselves alone in any situation. Let me rephrase it for you and you can use this cliché and I'll be happy with you. "Nothing ever will happen that God and you can't handle together." Whatever situation we find ourselves in, we can always remind ourselves that with God's help, we can get through it because that's what this passage is talking about. It's talking about how God carried Jesus through the difficulties of life. It's reminding us how God is for us in every situation. There isn't a situation you can be in that God will not be with you, carrying you, leading you, directing you, giving you the strength that you need to get through that particular situation. It's not a matter of being given a task that you can handle, it's about God being present and handling anything that falls upon you.

You see, it all comes down to that last portion of the eighth chapter where Paul does such a great summation. I love Paul's writing because you know sometimes, he goes overboard a little bit and that's okay. He runs through that whole litany of things that could possibly separate us from the love of God and he just keeps adding more things that prove his point. Whenever I read this passage, I just picture Paul sitting there writing this out and he goes "Oh and this can't separate us, no wait one more thing that can't separate us, nope wait one more thing that can't..." As he keeps coming up with a litany of things that some people might think could separate us from the love of God but then it simply dawns on him, "there's nothing in all of creation than can separate us from the love of God." You see he went through that whole litany of possibilities of things that could separate us from God to say nope, nope, nope, nope and he gets to the end and says just in case I missed anything let me make this clear there's NOTHING, nothing that can separate us from the love of God. That's the point of the eighth chapter of Romans that he wants us to see. That no matter what the situation. No matter how dire the times. No matter how difficult things may be. No matter how discouraged things we might feel. No matter how low our lives might feel. Even when we can't even figure out how to pray, God is there. And if God is for us what difference does anything else make. If God is for us what difference does it matter if anybody else is against us? That's the love from which we cannot be separated. That's the love that is ever present with us holding us up, carrying us along, bearing us when we need to be carried. Walking side by side with us when we're able to walk on our own strength. We have that love. We have that love which is so deep and broad, so rich and so pure, then what difference does anything else make? That's what Paul wants us to see and Paul would know. This is one of the last things that Paul ever wrote and his was not an easy lot in life, so he knew what he was speaking of and he's sharing from his heart to all of our hearts about what really matters in life. And what really matters is having God in our hearts, his love abiding with us, his spirit ever present with us, taking care of us day in and day out.

Would you pray with me? Almighty and ever-loving God what a great gift it is that you have given to us, an immeasurable gift, the gift of your love. A gift freely given, a gift that nothing in this world or the world yet to come could ever steal away from us. O heavenly father remind us in our hearts and in our lives that if we have that love everything else is secondary. We pray this in Jesus' name and for his sake. Amen.

Cross Purposes
Luke 24:25-33

September 8, 2019

There is nothing like jumping back into the thick of things after enjoying some time away! The text that stands before us today is one which is challenging in our first hearing and probably most of us just turn away from it because it doesn't sound like Jesus at all! When did Jesus ever teach anyone to hate? And why this talk about suffering? He bore the cross so I wouldn't have to! Why would he want me to suffer with him? Let's take a look at this passage and see what we might be missing.

It is an awkward passage, isn't it? It is difficult for us to hear the words flowing from Jesus' mouth. We know these must be words that Jesus spoke because no writer trying to attract people to the person and work of Jesus Christ would ever include this story out of a writer's imagination. This has to be something Jesus said but why?

First, I think we need to see that we have one of those Greek to English issues. Our English vocabulary is limited in many ways. I've talked with you before about the weakness of the word love in English compared with the three words the Greek vocabulary has. This is another one that is a struggle for the translator. We have love and we have hate. That seems to be the choice we are faced with. But there is more of a variable in the Greek. The word translated hate really doesn't seem to have a true counterpart in English. William Barclay, the Scottish Biblical scholar of a generation ago, proposes that we ought to translate it as love less. He proposes and I agree that what Jesus is saying is a matter of priorities. Where is the center of your focus? Jesus is trying to tell his followers that there is more than just being a follower - he is looking for disciples who will make His way their way. He is calling for disciples who will Love God more than self - who will love God more than any self-interest we may have.

I heard the story told of a professor who was greeted by a man, who said, "My son is a student of yours." The professor wryly replied, "He attends my lectures, but he is not a student of mine." You can be a follower without being a disciple. When I was in the Seminary, there were any number of Professors that I took classes from, not because I wanted to but because they were required. There were exceptions to this as well. Two of my favorites were Dr. Bruce Manning Metzger, the finest New Testament Scholar of his time, a well-known scholar and the other was Dr. Cullen I K Story the Professor of New Testament who taught Greek to the students. While, it is fair to say that I was not nor ever would be a language scholar, I took every course from Dr. Story, I could fit into my schedule. He was an amazing person. Before the incoming class entered the seminary, he would take all of their applications and read them, memorize details about each of us and remembering us from the picture we included with our application. This was well over 125 students every year! First time I met him, he called me by name and asked me questions based upon the information included in that application! But it was more than that, his care and concern for each of us was warm and loving. And when he opened up his Greek New Testament, you felt as if he was talking about an old friend when he spoke of the person of Jesus Christ. Can you see why I took every course I could from him? When I left the Seminary, I kept in touch with him right up to his death. I wanted to be learned from him, I wanted to be like him. I was a student of Cullen I K Story!

That is the distinction Jesus is trying to make. He doesn't want to have people who just like hearing his well told stories. Jesus wants people who want to be like Jesus with their lives. He knows that to be a disciple of Jesus Christ means that He is the highest priority of our lives. It doesn't mean that we can't love others, in fact we are called to love others, but that love is based in our love being empowered by the love of Jesus Christ.

You see, Jesus wants us to see that being a follower of Jesus Christ isn't enough. He needs us to make a true commitment. That's why he says we need to pick up our cross and follow Him. Now, don't misunderstand this. I have heard the phrase, "This is my cross to bear" so many times in my life. Virtually every single one of those times was a misinterpretation of what Jesus meant when he challenged us to pick up our cross and follow Him. I have heard people humorously introduce me to a spouse by saying, "I'd like you to meet my cross to bear." Other times I have heard people lament some chronic condition they endure by saying, "I guess this is my cross to bear." Do we really think that Jesus was trying to tell us that in order to be a true disciple of His that we needed to find some way to be miserable? Not a chance!

When Jesus is calling us to pick up our cross to be his true followers, he is making an analogy for us to see. For Jesus, to pick up his cross was not about finding an ultimate way to suffer but in reality, it was his ultimate act of love and selflessness. The importance of the cross of Jesus Christ isn't the pain he endured - it is the love that he exhibited. If he didn't love us, he wouldn't have picked up that cross. If he was self-centered, he would have walked away from the Garden of Gethsemane. The best way I know how to describe the meaning of the cross is to say that in that moment absolute love clashed with absolute evil. It seemed as if evil won but we know that the absolute love of the Triune God conquered the worst evil had to offer.

"Pick up your cross and follow me" are not words of suffering for Christ's sake. "Pick up your cross and follow me" are words of encouragement. They are words of challenge. They are words that are meant to draw the best out of who we are. They are words that embolden us to put ourselves to the side and put the love of God to the front of who we are and all we do.

Jesus wasn't looking for people who would stand on the sidelines and cheer him on. He wasn't looking for people who would pat him on the back and say, "Atta boy!" A cursory reading of the Gospels will show you that he already had plenty of people who wanted to see him work miracles, preach a good sermon and certainly there was no shortage of those who wanted Him to do something special for them from healings, to those who wanted him to conquer the Roman authorities and even his closest friends wanted to ask the favor of receiving high positions in the coming Kingdom. There was and still is no shortage of those who want something from Jesus.

The core of this whole teaching of Jesus is simply his desire to have people who are willing to change their central focus from self to

God. He wants, to this day, people who are willing to be true disciples of Jesus Christ. If He is asking to you to love less all that you hold dear, if He is asking you to pick up your cross to follow Him, it is because he wants you to walk in his way of love. He is challenging each one of us to live a life that is like His. He is seeking disciples who will be His people in this crazy mixed up world of ours. He is calling you and me to have a deep heartfelt desire to be more like Jesus in every way of our lives.

Will you pray with me? Oh one who has shown us what love truly is, we confess that this earthly world has many attractions for us. We are drawn away from you so easily. Help us in our weakness to love you more and this world less. Help us to pick up the cross of love so that we might live selfless lives like Jesus. In Christ's name we pray. Amen

The Road from Ephesus—United in Love
Ephesians 5: 15-21

February 7, 2010

We continue in our study of the Book of Ephesians: the letter to the
church of Ephesus. And we look today in the fifth chapter to verses
15-21, a very appropriate text for us in the living of our lives.
Ephesians 5 beginning with verse 15:

> *"Be careful then how you live, not as unwise but as wise, 16 make the
> most of every opportunity because the days are evil. Therefore do not be
> foolish but understand what the Lord's will is. 18 Do not get drunk on
> wine, which leads to debauchery; instead be filled with the Spirit.
> Speak to one another with psalms and hymns and spiritual songs, sing
> and make music in your heart to the Lord, always giving thanks to
> God the Father for everything in the name of our Lord Jesus Christ.
> Submit to one another out of reverence for Christ."*

May the Lord bless this a portion from his holy word.

I have to admit that there are things that I do plan well but more
often than not there are things that I do not plan well. And today is
one of those days that I did not plan well. You see I do my sermon
preparation well ahead. I try to look forward to the year ahead and
to ponder what text and what topics that the Lord is wanting me to
present before you. And so I try to line out all of the different series
of sermons and the texts that I'll be preaching on as I look ahead for
the year. As I do that, I try to keep in mind all of the great days of
the church and of the faith that we have and make those special, like
Christmas and Easter and Thanksgiving and all those wonderful
holidays that we celebrate. But somewhere along the line I kind of
goofed up on today. I forgot that today is the high holy day, Super
Bowl Sunday. And I have to ask the question of what kind of
preacher preaches on this text from Ephesians on Super Bowl
Sunday – "be not drunk with wine." But it was pointed out to me
that there's nothing in the text about beer. I don't think Paul

intended that loophole to be there so please do keep that in mind today.

You know my sense of humor and you know my mind takes me to funny places, so as I was reading this text in preparation for today and I thought, "you know let's take this text extremely seriously". This text goes on to talk about how we ought to spend time together singing songs and hymns and praise music and I thought well let's really get the point across on this text today and say "okay everybody I'm going to make it mandatory that we all come back here at kick-off time and gather in the sanctuary for a hymn sing." But then I had a hunch that I just might not fill the sanctuary if I did that. I thought I would probably be pretty lonely singing all by myself.

This is a marvelous text and it is a good one for us to consider in our hearts and minds even on an unofficial national holiday. How is it that we live our lives? In all seriousness I don't think that Paul is calling for us to not enjoy the good things of life. We know that for 90% of us Super Bowl Sunday isn't about who wins or who loses. It's just a chance to be together and to enjoy family and friends. For many of us it is a chance to eat all the foods that we normally feel guilty about eating but today we'll give ourselves a waiver on that. Although, as a parenthetical remark, we really ought to be pulling for the Indianapolis Colts since their quarterback, Peyton Manning, is a Presbyterian elder. So we Presbyterians really need to be pulling for him today. If you haven't chosen a team to pull for today you can pull for Peyton Manning as a Presbyterian elder, Second Presbyterian Church in Indianapolis, Indiana. In case you wanted to know what, his credentials were, and he can throw a football too.

I don't think Paul wants us to give up the fun things. Paul was one, as you read through all of his writings, who had a wonderful sense of humor. He did seem to enjoy life. I don't think he would want us to choose to become the philosophical ascetics: people who don't enjoy life, people who don't have pleasure or people who don't enjoy the great things that make life so meaningful. Paul was not ascetic by any means and was not one who would have us give up all those sorts of things that are good for us. It's good to be together with family and friends. It's good to have celebrations whatever the occasion may be. Whether it's Super Bowl Sunday, Thanksgiving

41

with the family or whatever the occasion may be, the Apostle Paul wants us to enjoy those things.

What he does want us to see is that in life we have opportunities. Every day that you and I get up in the morning is a day filled with opportunities. Every day when we get up in the morning, we are given the opportunity to make choices of how we're going to live this day, this gift that God has given to us. The Apostle Paul wants us to know that we are given these choices and that we need to make wise choices. He's calling for us to live lives that are wise and not foolish, to make good choices and not bad. He uses an interesting phrase in here and a phrase that when you first read it is kind of a head scratcher. It's one of those ones that you wonder what in the world he means. He says, "for the days are evil" and you go "huh?" What does he mean the days are evil? What's he trying to say to us there and what he is trying to communicate to us? What we hear, if we don't over read that phrase, is that each day that we have we have choices between good and evil. We can choose between what is right and choosing what is wrong. We have the choice every day of doing that which is good and true and beautiful. We are able to do that which is enriching for those around us, something that edifies our family and friends. We can choose to make this world a better place or we can choose to do that which is not so good. We can choose to produce bad results.

Why did the Apostle Paul say, "do not be drunk with wine?" It wasn't because he didn't enjoy a glass of wine. In his writing to Timothy, he directs Timothy to raise a glass of wine and to enjoy it as a medicinal thing to help his stomach. So it's not like the Apostle Paul is opposed to wine or anything of that sort. What he was opposed to was what wine can do to us, what alcohol can do to us. It can hamper our decision-making ability and we might tend to choose wrong when we are drunk. Alcohol will do that. What he's trying to say to us is that life is full of choices between good and evil, between doing what is right and doing what is wrong. Choose what is right!

I'll never forget that during the time we were doing our flood relief work, there was a fellow in the community who was harassing some of our volunteers and he said that they were stupid. He said that nobody should give up their time to help somebody else. Let them fend for themselves. I couldn't believe he said that. I couldn't believe he said that but that was his attitude. In his life he chose one avenue. He chose an avenue that was self-centered and an avenue that didn't give a rip about anybody else. He chose a way of living that was all about himself. If it didn't gain something for himself then he wasn't going to be bothered with it. But as Christians, as followers of Jesus Christ, as ones who have experienced God's love in our hearts and in our lives, we know that there's a better choice to be made. We can choose to be loving. We can choose to be gracious. We can choose to be kind. We can choose to be forgiving. We can choose to be the kind of people that God wants us to be selfless and giving, caring and compassionate. Each day of our lives comes with choices and the Apostle Paul wants us to choose that which is good, to do God's will in our lives, to live lives that are loving and caring and gracious. That's what he's asking us to do, to make good wise decisions, to choose good over evil, to choose selflessness over selfishness. How shall we choose this day? Amen.

The Road from Ephesus—Being Prepared

Ephesians 6: 10-18

February 14, 2010

Today is the last Sunday before we enter into the season of Lent and so today also is the last Sunday that we will be looking at the letter to the church at Ephesus in the sixth chapter today. We'll read Ephesians 6 beginning with verse 10 through verse 18:

> *Finally, be strong in the Lord and in his mighty power. Put on the full armor of God so you can take your stand against the devil's schemes. For our struggle is not against flesh and blood but against the rulers, against the authorities, against the powers of this dark world and against the spiritual forces of evil in the heavenly realms. Therefore put on the full armor of God so when the day of evil comes you may be able to stand your ground. And after you've done everything, just stand. Stand firm then with the belt of truth buckled around your waist with a breastplate of righteousness in place, with your feet fitted with the readiness that comes from the gospel of peace. In addition to all this, take up the shield of faith with which you can extinguish all the flaming arrows of the evil one. Take the helmet of salvation and the sword of the spirit which is the word of God. And pray in the spirit in all occasions with all kinds of prayers and requests. With this in mind, be alert and always keep on praying for all the saints.*

May the Lord bless this a portion from his holy word.

This is an interesting passage of scripture. It is one that, in some sense of the word, has fallen out of favor within the Christian church. It is one that for many years was a popular text to be preached upon and actually made its mark in the church in a number of different ways. Last summer in our travels we were in a great cathedral church in New Jersey. As Debby and I were going through this beautiful gothic cathedral building, I saw that they had a series of beautiful stained-glass windows there. Each of these beautiful windows depicted one of the armaments that are listed in this passage from the sixth chapter of Ephesians. But over the years, over the past 30, maybe even 40 years now, we've grown a little uncomfortable with this passage of scripture.

I think that's for a couple of different reasons. First and foremost I believe we're really uncomfortable with the imagery of battlement as a Christian imagery. We like to think of ourselves as being peaceable people, people who try to practice peace in our lives and we try to live our lives as Christians in a spirit of love and grace. "Blessed are the Peacemakers", after all. So to have this kind of imagery is in a very real sense bothersome to us. We're not comfortable with talking about putting on the full armor of God, the breastplate of righteousness, the buckle of truth, the helmet of faith. All these kind of embattlement imageries are uncomfortable to us. We don't like to think that way. We don't like to imagine ourselves as being warriors or people who are ready to do battle. That's not the way we want to see ourselves. We are peaceable, kind, gentle people. That's how we envision what it means to be a Christian: we're kind and gentle and loving. That's what we're striving for, that's what we're seeking to be with our lives. We read a passage like this and we just begin to cringe a little bit because of its discomfort to us, putting on battle armament, putting on the armor of God all that just makes us very uncomfortable. It's really difficult for us to picture ourselves in that way so we have a tendency simply to ignore it and I understand that. I appreciate it and I am too, a little uncomfortable with this passage but I think if we can get around that discomfort, if we can get around that kind of idea of what it means and we can see what the writer wanted us to see, then I think we can find something there that we need for the living of our lives.

You see, I think that what we're being taught here is that being a Christian is hard work. It's not an easy task. It is, in a sense, a battle that we wage. It is an ongoing effort on our parts to do what we're called to do. Being a Christian is not something that is easy, and we all know that life is never fair to us. Life is difficult to us both in that what happens accidentally and those things that happen to us purposely. We're hurt, we're harmed. Life can be very difficult. Trust me, I wish that weren't true. I mean I've been looking for a lot of years for that passage in the Bible where Jesus says to be a Christian, to be a follower of his means you draw a bye on all of life's pains. I've been looking for that passage where he promises us that to follow him would be a walk through the rose garden. I've been looking for those loopholes for a lot of years and I haven't found a single loophole yet. And what we're being told here is that life is challenging and to be a Christian makes life even more challenging because we're going against the stream of the world. We're going against the way the world would have us to go. We are marching to a different drummer and that makes life even more difficult.

What the writer's trying to help us to see is that we called to take upon us what God offers to us. That as we go through all the difficulties of life, as we go through the challenges of life, as we go through the pain and turmoil and the suffering and the sorrows of life, that we don't do it on our own strength. Because if you look at all these armaments which are being offered in this passage from Ephesians, we'll see that each one of them is a gift from God, his righteousness, his strength. These are not things that are of our own ability, these are not things that we need to do. We are called to accept these gifts from God to allow him to surround us with his strength, to fill us with his righteousness, to allow him to be that guardian who is with us every step along the way.

No matter how difficult life gets we have that promise that in wrapping ourselves in God, we'll get through it. I love how he phrases this, that when you get through everything, you stand. You know, it's not like you're going to jump, it's not like you're going to run, it's not going to be some great exhibition of our strength, but to get through all of the struggles and the sorrows and the pain of life, to get through it and be able to stand. That's what we're striving for and that's what he's promising for us is that gift of his strength to surround us and to hold us up when we just can't seem to stand on our own.

I think the second element that we're uncomfortable with is the thought of evil. We don't like to think about evil in the world, do we? We prefer to think about the goodness of the world, we like to think about all of those positive things and that's not bad. That's not bad to focus in on the positive. But sometimes you have to see that there is evil in the world. I'll always remember, when I was doing a year of interim ministry in the Lackawanna County jail in Scranton, PA, that there was this fellow who came in one Sunday for chapel services there. Now you have to picture this, the chapel in the Lakawanna County jail was a very small room. That whole room was probably half the size of this chancel area up here and they would put about 40 or so prisoners in there. Then they would put me in there, Bible in hand and then they'd lock the door! They didn't want them to get out, but they didn't think about the fact that I just might want to get out! They assured me that they were always right outside the door, but I didn't know that to be true or not to be true. So you can picture my fear.

I start to get to know some of the guys in the jail there and was starting to get comfortable with a number of them and developing a relationship with them and it was going along quite well. Then this one Sunday, this mountain of a man comes in. He must have been 6'9"or 6'10" and built like he was an NFL linebacker. But what really scared me was that he sat there during the whole service just staring at me. I couldn't get done with that service quick enough. I just wanted to get out of that room in a hurry. After the service I said to one of the guards, "who was that new fellow, the big guy?" He said, "Oh that fellow, he murdered his family down in Philadelphia. He took an axe to his parents and his sisters." I said, "What's he doing here?" The guard answered, "well, he was supposed to be on his way to Fairview, the hospital for the criminally insane but they didn't have the paperwork done correctly so the sheriff from Philadelphia County left him with us until they got the paperwork done. That way they wouldn't have to bring him all the way back to Philadelphia and come back up again." I thought, thank you very much. That was very nice of them! I'm glad you told me beforehand, so I wasn't nervous. But I looked at that prisoner and I looked in his eyes and I just knew there was a story there because there was a chill that came over me. I knew that there was something evil about that man.

So there is evil. I've seen it. I've known it. We've all experienced it in some way, some fashion and what we're promised in this text is God's presence. In the battle in this world between good and evil, we seek to do good, we seek to be loving, we seek to be kind, we seek to be generous, we seek to be faithful, we seek to be all of these things as followers of Jesus Christ. That is a battle of good versus evil. We're seeking to be good and to do good in this world and we're promised in the midst of that challenge that God will surround us, cover us with those armaments, that armor of his love, that protection of his faithfulness, the righteousness of who he is righteous will be upon us. But we have to allow him to do that. We have to accept that gift into our lives, to allow him to surround us, to cover us, to protect us, to be with us every step along the way. It's a choice that we need to make. Do we choose to go through this life with all of its troubles and trials, trying to do it on our own strength or do we choose to allow God to carry us, to hold us up and to get us through. That's the choice. That's the choice we need to make. Amen.

Let's bow our heads in prayer. Almighty and ever-loving God, we seem to want to do everything by our own strength. We seem to want to do everything by our own ability, by our own power. Call it pride, call it will, call it whatever you wish but it doesn't get us very far. Lord we seek your presence. We ask that you would enfold us in your love and in your protection that as we seek to be your people to do your work, to do acts of goodness in this world, that you would protect us and hold us up in your ever caring hands. We pray this in Jesus' name and for his sake. Amen.

The Church is Legalistic

Galatians 3:1-9

June 8, 2014

We continue on this Pentecost Day to explore and to look at some of the misperceptions that people have about the Christian church. Some of the myths and misperceptions that people believe about the Christian church are somewhat based in their experience. It is also possible that there may be a little bit of truth in them. It very well may be that we as the Christian church have brought some of these problems upon ourselves. One of the ones that is a little bit irksome to me, but I understand where it comes from, is the phrase that I've heard on a number of occasions. Any number of people have said to me that they didn't want to be part of the church because the church is all about legalism. It's all about the do's and the don'ts. It's all about the rules and the regulations and mostly about the don'ts. There's a misperception out there that the church sits around and makes up rules because we're afraid somebody somewhere is having fun.

But that's not who we are, is it? That's not the nature of the church so let's take a look. Let's go back to the pages of the scriptures and let's go back to the days of the early church. We recognize even then that was a question, an issue that they were dealing with even in the early years of Christianity. And I'm only going to read a few short verses from the third chapter of Galatians, but I would encourage you in this week ahead to read through the entire book of Galatians. It's not very long. It's a very short book in the Bible but it is important because Galatians is all about this question of law verses freedom. I think Paul does a wonderful job of helping us to understand where we ought to land. Let me just share with you this portion from the third chapter, the first nine verses.

> *"You foolish Galatians! Who has bewitched you? It was before your eyes that Jesus was publically exhibited as crucified. The only thing I want to learn from you is this. Did you receive the Spirit by doing the works of the law, or by believing what you heard? Are you so foolish?*

49

Having started with the Spirit are you now ending with the flesh? Did you experience so much for nothing if it really was for nothing? Well then, does God supply you with the Spirit and work miracles among you by you doing the works of the law or by your believing what you heard? Just as Abraham "believed God, and it was reckoned to him as righteousness," so, you see, those who believe are the descendants of Abraham. And the scripture foreseeing that God would justify the Gentiles by faith, declared the gospel beforehand to Abraham, saying, "All the Gentiles shall be blessed in you." For this reason, those who believe are blessed with Abraham who believed."

May the Lord bless this a portion from his Holy word.

A number of years ago I attended a seminar which was actually mandatory for all of us ministers in the Presbytery where I once served. It was a day-long seminar on sexual harassment and sexual boundaries for ministers to learn You know what that all encompasses. So we sat there for eight hours listening to the presenter giving all these rationales, descriptions and explanations and so on. It was not a fun day. It was a very long day. First of all the speaker spoke in a monotone voice, so that didn't help any at all, but we got through it. The fellow that I drove up with, as he and I were riding back home together, he turns to me and says, "Don't you think Steve it would have been a lot easier if they just told us what we could and couldn't do?"

Well there is something in human nature, there is something in our humanness that likes to have rules, likes to have things set out for us. There is something inside of us where we like to know what the boundaries are. We like to know the rights from wrongs. We like to know what we're allowed to do and what we're prohibited from doing. We find a certain comfort in the law. There is something that is comforting for us in the law. I know I'm not any different than anybody else. My family will tell you that if I'm driving on the interstate and I haven't seen a speed limit sign for a while, I get nervous. I do. I get nervous. It's like "what if it changed back to 55 and I didn't notice and I'm still doing 70?" And I get all nervous until I see the next speed limit sign and I think, "ok, I'm good." You know I'm this way because there is something comforting, something that puts us at ease if we have that law and it's clearly delineated for us. It is set out there and we know what the parameters of that law are. We all know that maybe we don't always follow them precisely, I mean, if it says 70, I might go a little bit above that. I might hit 72 or 73. But at least I know what the boundaries are, and I try and stay close to those parameters. There is something in our human nature that likes to have those boundaries. We like to have those rules spelled out for us. We want to know when to cross the T's and when to dot the I's. There is something that is comfortable for us in that. It's always been that way! If you go back in the pages of scripture and read about, you'll hear about the Pharisees, a wonderful people. I know they kind of get a bad rap. They really shouldn't. They were wonderful people – they were the kind of people whom you would like to have living next door to you because they were the ones that mowed their lawns regularly, made sure their house was painted every few years and they kept their property up beautifully. They would make wonderful neighbors to have around you. They found such comfort in the law that they tried to make sure they had every contingency covered.

They would take a simple rule, a simple law such as "keep the Sabbath holy." You know it, it's one of the Ten Commandments, very straight forward, keep the Sabbath holy. It's a day that should be set aside for worship of God and praise of God and to rest and refresh ourselves. Simple law. But they would take that law and they would carry it out to the ninth degree. They would raise every possible scenario and try and come up with an answer for that. For instance, if you were a Pharisee and you had an animal and that animal of yours fell into the well on your property on the Sabbath, could you rescue that animal? Would that be working on the Sabbath? Nobody has a guess for me. Okay. The answer, wait, did I hear a guess? Yes? Okay, I got a few yeses. The answer is yes and no. They made it so complicated: if you had an animal and it fell into the well, if the animal's nose is above water, the animal had to wait until the Sabbath was over to be rescued. If the animal's nose was below water, you were allowed to rescue it on the Sabbath. That's how fine-tuned they try to make everything. They tried to make everything so that there was no issue, there was no gray areas. Everything they tried to make into a black and white issue. And see, that still carries on. There are those places and those churches that still like to have everything spelled out in black and white.

When I was in the Wyalusing church, across the river in Terrytown, there was a small Baptist church there. The pastor of that church, I wouldn't have known it, but he put a letter to the editor in the local newspaper delineating the 32 things you had to do to be a Christian. I read that and I thought it was the most horrible thing I'd ever read in my life. He delineated so many things and most them excluded me from being a Christian. For instance, back in that day I actually had the ability to grow hair and occasionally it did touch my collar and did go over my ears and that was precluded. He wrote that in order to be a Christian you had to have hair that did not touch your collar and did not touch your ears. I've also had a beard my entire adult life and if you had facial hair you were excluded from being a Christian. You had to have clean-shaven and your sideburns could not touch the opening in your ear. If that wasn't bad enough all the things for women were even worse. In order to be a Christian in his church the women could not leave their homes unless they wore a dress that touched the ground. It had to touch the ground. They could never get their hair cut, their hair had to be untouched – could not be cut, could not be curled, could not have anything with it. They could not wear make-up or anything else like that, no adornment, no earrings, no jewelry! A simple wedding band was the only jewelry they were allowed to wear. This pastor had delineated everything within his church and every member of that church was expected to follow every single one of those rules in order to be baptized and become a member of that congregation. And if you weren't baptized and a member of that congregation you were not considered in his thinking to be a Christian.

So we do have that tendency to try to delineate fully and completely. We make rules for every situation. It was no different in the early church because Paul is writing to the church of Galatia and he's upset with them twice in this one short passage. He refers to them as foolish people because they have fallen back into that trap. They've fallen back into that trap of trying to make a rule for everything and fit every situation into a rule. He says to them, "who bewitched you? Who dazzled you? Who put a spell on you to make you think that how you live your life is going to earn God's love? That's not the gospel! That's not the gospel we preach. We preach the gospel of Jesus Christ crucified, Jesus Christ raised from dead that it is by believing in Jesus that our salvation comes to us, not by our actions, not by our deeds." He asked them the question, "who of you thinks that you can earn God's love by living a perfect life? You've given up something good and generous for something that is a burden and will weigh you down and wear you out."

The church by its nature, by God's design, by the gift of the Holy Spirit, the church is not a place of rules and regulations. It is not a place of perfect people living perfectly well. It is a place for real people to live real lives as forgiven people. The Church is people who know that we are loved by God, not because of anything we have done; not because we have followed all of the rules; not because we have crossed all the T's and dotted all the I's, but because of what God has done for us through his Son Jesus Christ. A gift freely given; a love generously shared with us. That's what the church celebrates. It is not a hotel for saints. The church is a hospital for sinners. We are imperfect people; we will remain imperfect people, but we live together as forgiven imperfect people.

You know I tried to find an analogy to help because I know the problem with a sermon like this is that sometimes you start to think "By golly, I can do anything I want. If God's going to forgive me for everything, I do then I'm going to go out and have a good time and I'm not going to worry about it." That's not what Paul is talking about in Galatians. He's talking about us not being burdened by the law but allowing the Holy Spirit to work in and through us to guide us in our decision making; to help us face each difficult question in our lives with the over-arching question of how can I be sharing God's love in this situation. How can I make God's love visible through my decisions that I make? So I was trying to come up with an analogy. I tried it earlier and they thought, maybe. So I'm going to try it with all of you too to see if you like this analogy or not because I'm trying to come up with a way to give us a visual picture of how this all works for us as Christians. A way to understand that we're not legalistic but we're not, at the same time, freewheeling on everything and doing anything and everything we want to, so I came up with this analogy. If you go to any of our wonderful shopping centers that we have around here, in almost every single one of them, as you drive along in front of the buildings, every so many feet there is a crosswalk and a stop sign. You can picture that, right? Virtually every one of those shopping plazas has one of those stop signs every so many feet. Now, if we are to live as legalistic people in our lives then we are like those who go through those parking lots, come to a complete stop at every one and look both ways and proceed. But there are those in their Christian lives want to go to the opposite extreme. Since we are forgiven people and we are not under the law anymore, we're going to drive through every stop sign no matter what. Full speed ahead, we have to get to the other end of the parking lot and we're going to get there fast. But I think what the apostle Paul is trying to help us to see is that there is an alternative, a middle way. We drive up to the stop sign, we slow down, we're cautious, we make sure nobody is there and we drive on. We don't have to come to a complete stop, but we are being very careful. We're following the spirit of the law maybe not the letter of the law. Does that help? Maybe not. I'm getting a lot of blank looks.

I'll keep trying to find a good analogy to help you understand what it is that we're called to do as Christians. Not to be burdened by the law, but to allow the law to guide us in our lives, to give us a foundation, to give us some broad parameters. Then the law doesn't become for us something that burdens us or something that we use as a means of earning God's love. It is for us, as John Calvin would say, an avenue of living in thanksgiving. That out of our gratitude for God, for the grace of his love for us, we seek to please him in all of our actions and in the way that we live our lives. Would you pray with me?

Almighty and ever-loving God, we do thank you for the gift of your Son, Jesus Christ, a gift freely given. A gift given to us while we were yet sinners, a gift given to us not because of who we are but in spite of who we are. We thank you for that grace. Help us to live our lives in response to that grace. To not allow ourselves to become burdened down with law but to allow the law to be for us a tool to help us to see how we might live our lives in faithful service to you. We pray this in Jesus' name, for his sake. Amen.

Journey with Jesus: Life's Goal
I Timothy 6: 6-19

September 26, 2010

The scripture text that I call to our attention today is found in Paul's first letter to Timothy. We continue in our brief study of first Timothy by looking today in the sixth chapter: the end of his letter. I don't know if you have experienced this like I have but often times when I'm visiting with someone and it is getting close to the time to leave, we actually get to the heart of the conversation. We seem to wait to the end of a conversation before we get to that important element that we wanted to make sure we talked about. We have that habit of saying a lot of things, then getting to what we really want to talk about in the first place. I think Paul is doing that in his letter to Timothy and to the church that Timothy served as a pastor. And so we'll read what he has to say, and we'll hear some wisdom and some truth that we need to hear in our lives. We'll kind of overhear a little bit of conversation between Paul and Timothy.

> *"But Godliness with contentment is great gain; for we brought nothing into the world, and we can take nothing out of it; but if we have food and clothing we will be content with that. People who want to get rich fall into temptation and into a trap and into many foolish and harmful desires that plunge men into ruin and destruction. For the love of money is a root of all kinds of evil; some people eager for money have wandered from the faith and pierced themselves with many griefs. But you, man of God, flee from all this; and pursue righteousness, godliness, faith, love, endurance and gentleness. Fight the good fight of the faith, take hold of the eternal life to which you were called when you made your good confession in the presence of many witnesses. In the sight of God who gives life to everything and of Christ Jesus while testifying before Pontius Pilate made the good confession. I charge you to keep this commandment, without spot or blame until the appearing of our Lord Jesus Christ: which God will bring about in his own time, God the blessed and only ruler, the King of kings and Lord of lords who alone is immortal, and who lives in unapproachable light; whom no one*

has seen or can see: to him be honor and might forever. Amen.
Command those who are rich in this present world, not to be arrogant,
nor to put their hope in wealth which is so uncertain, but to put their
hope God who richly provides us everything for our enjoyment;
command them to do good, to be rich in good deeds and be willing to
share. In this way they will lay up treasure themselves in a firm
foundation for the coming age so they may take hold of the life that is
truly life."

May the Lord bless this a portion from his holy word.

A couple of years ago I was meeting with a young couple helping
them get prepared for their wedding day. As I was helping them
prepare, we were going through the order of worship for the
wedding service. I was trying to go through it and explain to them
the different elements so they could get the most meaning out of it.
I wanted them to clearly understand what promises they were
making, and I wanted them to understand all of the service so it
would be rich for them. As I'm going through, I came to one part,
and I said, "now this is where I will give you the charge." As I said
that I saw the bride's eyes go wide open, so I stopped! I was kind of
confused why she was looking at me like that and then she said, "can
I ask you a question?" I said, "yes, please do." She said, "you're
going to go through the whole wedding service and you're going to
get to this point and then you're going to ask me for the fees?" She
thought the "charge" was the fees for the wedding, but a "charge" is
that gift from one to another of some insight, some wisdom, some
desire to help the other people. In the wedding service the "charge"
is that part of the service where one challenges the bride and groom
to grow into the new state in which they find themselves. It's a
challenge or a bit of last-minute advice to help them to have the best
marriage possible.

The Apostle Paul in writing to Timothy is doing what a lot of older
pastors have done for younger pastors over the years. There is a
tradition we have within our Presbyterian system. When we ordain
a young pastor or when we install a new pastor, we have as a part of
that service a charge to the pastor: a challenge, a sharing of wisdom
from one generation to another generation. And that's what the
Apostle Paul is trying to do here in his words to Timothy as a young

pastor of a church. He's trying to help Timothy to avoid some of the pitfalls that he has seen others fall into. Therefore, as he is concluding his letter to Timothy, he comes to this charge to Timothy to not fall into this pattern of life that has happened to some in the early church. It seems to me that the more things change, the more they stay the same. You might not believe this but in the early church, money was an issue. Can you believe that they had problems? Can you believe they never had enough money to do everything they wanted to do? Yet, that was the problem and it was happening in the early church.

We read about this in James and we see it elsewhere, that when there would be people coming into the church who dressed a little bit nicer or who were known to have a few more resources, those people were given seats of honor. They were elevated over the rest of the people who might not have had any resources. But the Apostle Paul saw where that led. He saw what was happening in the early church and he didn't want Timothy and his church to fall into that same trap where money became the goal, where money became the object for how one lived one's life. He didn't want them to fall into that trap where we seek to find our hope and our security in how much we have accumulated. He didn't want us to fall into that trap where we find the meaning and purpose in our lives based upon how successful we are in a worldly point of view. He didn't want us to fall into that trap where we trusted our bank accounts more than we trusted our God. Do you see what was happening in the early church? Paul saw what was happening. He knew what would happen and he said to Timothy, "you've got to understand that the love of money is the root of so much evil. That when possessions, when money becomes that about which we are passionate, when having these things become the desires of our hearts over and above everything and anything else, then that leads us into a trap that brings us heartache and takes us away from that which is truly good, that which is truly lasting, that being God's love and grace in each of our lives." Paul saw this happening and he didn't want Timothy to fall into that trap so he's giving him this charge, this wisdom, this advice from one generation to another, to avoid that trap. Don't allow possessions to become the priorities of your lives. Don't allow money and things like that to become the passion of your hearts.

Look out for, seek after righteousness, gentleness, love, all of those good things that we see and find in Jesus Christ. Those should be the focus. Those should be the goals of our lives, not how much we can accumulate, not how much we can have in the bank account. There is no security in that. You know that. You've seen that.

I know, as I am talking to you today, I know that all of you are out there thinking well does that mean money is no good. No, he goes on to say that it's how you use what you have that's important. He says for those of you who are rich in the fellowship, those of you who have resources, practice generosity. He quotes Jesus in this, "store up for yourselves treasure in heaven." You know what Jesus said. It can't be rusted away; it can't be stolen. Those treasures that we have in heaven are permanent. That's how we should live our lives! If we have riches in our lives, we should practice generosity. We should be open and eager to share with others. I know you're sitting there going, well that's all well and good Steve but I'm not rich. Anybody here want to admit to being rich?

The fact of the matter is this. We're all rich. How many of us have a home to go to after the service today? How many of us have a refrigerator with some food in it? How many of us have a pantry with a couple of cans of soup and bag of potato chips? How many of us have a car to get ourselves from here to there? If you've answered yes to any of those questions, you're richer than 90% of the people in this world. We forget how blessed we are. We forget how blessed we are to live in this great nation of the United States of America. We forget that in the United States we talk about hunger while other countries are dealing with starvation. We talk about poverty while other countries are talking about survival. We are the rich people. We are the people that God has blessed. We are the people that Paul was warning Timothy - do not fall into the trap of thinking that our meaning, our purpose, our lives, our security, are found in our possessions. The Apostle Paul warned you and me when he was talking to Timothy to live our lives in such a way that our passion, our desires are not for possessions but that our passion be for Jesus Christ and his love, his church, all of the people in this world that he loves us so dearly.

Now if I take you for a little drive down into the country, down in Pennsylvania in the hills of Central PA there's a number of little towns on the edge of the anthracite coal mining region, places like Lopez and Bernice and Mildred. And if I took you to this one particular town down there: Lopez PA. If I took you there and you looked around you would think this is a God-forsaken town. The houses in their glory days were hardly anything but shacks. Most of those houses you and I would not be comfortable living in. But if I took you to that town and drove you up on the hillside there, we would find a little Russian Orthodox Church. As you and I would go into that little chapel on the hillside there we would open the doors and I would bet that your jaws would drop. The artwork is incredibly beautiful, the iconography is absolutely amazing. The gilded work – breathtaking. In that little hardscrabble town, in that town where you look at them and say they didn't have two nickels to rub together, they saw that a priority in their lives was building and maintaining a place where they could all pray to God their glory, their thanks, and their praise. They saw that they needed a place to be reminded of what is important and what is not. They made decisions, they made choices, they made sacrifices to give God the glory.

In each of our lives we make decisions day in and day out, we make choices within our lives as to what is our highest priority. Paul is giving us a clear-cut choice whether our highest priority will be the things of this world or will our highest priority be serving and loving a God who has loved and served us through his son, Jesus Christ. Amen.

Let's bow our heads and pray. Almighty and ever-loving God, you have so richly blessed us. You have blessed us immeasurably well. Father, sometimes we lose our focus. Sometimes we think that it's the stuff that matters and when we do that, we allow that to cloud our vision and we forget to see that you are our all-in-all. You are our hope and security. You are where we find our worth and our purpose. O gracious Lord help us to have clear vision and clear priorities in our lives so that our one and only goal is to love you and to serve you with our lives. We pray this in Jesus' name, Amen.

A Proper Perspective
Deuteronomy 26: 1-11

February 21, 2010

As we enter into the season of Lent, it is a good opportunity for us to ponder in our hearts, to think about where we have come from, to consider where we ought to be, to ponder where we should go with our lives. And so it is that we take a look back. We go back to the pages of the Old Testament, the book of Deuteronomy very early in the history of the people of God. And we look at the 26th chapter of Deuteronomy to this very telling passage of scripture.

> *"When you have entered the land that the Lord your God is giving you as an inheritance and have taken possession of it and settled in it, take some of the first fruits of all that you produce from the soil of the land the Lord your God has given you and put them in a basket and go to the place that the Lord your God will choose as a dwelling for his name and say to the priest and office at that time, "I declare today to the Lord your God that I have come to the land the Lord swore to our forefathers to give us." The priest shall take the basket from your hands and set it down on the altar of the Lord your God. Then you shall declare before the Lord your God, "my father was a wandering Aramean and he went down into Egypt with a few people and lived there and became a great nation, powerful and numerous. But the Egyptians mistreated us and made us suffer, putting us to hard labor. Then we cried out to the Lord, the God of our fathers; the Lord heard our voice and saw our misery, our toil, and our oppression. So the Lord brought us out of Egypt with a mighty hand and an outstretched arm, with great terror and miraculous signs and wonders; he brought us to this place and gave us this land, a land flowing with milk and honey. And now I bring the first of the fruit of the soil that you, O Lord, have given me." Place the basket before the Lord your God and bow down before him and you and the Levites and the aliens among you shall rejoice in all the good things the Lord your God has given to you and to your household."*

May the Lord bless this a portion of his holy word.

I get a kick out of the fact that whenever there's a religious holiday or a religious season, the newspaper and the television news programs always try to find something religious to put in the paper or to broadcast. I guess they feel there must be an obligation to do something religious every now and then in the course of the year. And this season that we have entered into is no exception. I saw on Ash Wednesday morning on the newscast that I was watching a story that they uncovered, probably because they were looking for something religious themed for Ash Wednesday, an incident about a young man who was separated from his wife. They were in the midst of a painful divorce and this young man was being interviewed because part of the agreement in their separation was an agreement that he would not take their three-year-old daughter to any service that was not of the Jewish faith. But what he did was he took his little girl to his home parish, a Roman Catholic Church, and had this child baptized and put it on YouTube so that everybody in the world knew about it. Of course, the lawyers are now involved in the situation as we speak. But it turns out that this young man himself is a lawyer and as he was being interviewed by the newscaster, the reporter said to him, "Now the agreement that you signed was that you wouldn't take your daughter into any house of worship that wasn't of the Jewish tradition." And this young lawyer said, "I didn't break the agreement." And the reporter kind of looked blankly at him and the lawyer went on and said, "The Christian church is a radical extension of the Jewish faith." And the reporter had no reply whatsoever. He was lost at that point.

What you have to understand about lawyers is that they never use a word unless it means exactly what they want it to mean. They choose their words wisely and carefully and they use them appropriately and at the appropriate time. So the key word for him was a "radical" part of the Jewish faith. When you and I hear the word radical we think of the 1960's. Long hair, back when I used to be able to grow long hair, beards, tie-dye t-shirts (you had to have your tie-dye shirt). There were marches and protests and love-ins. That's what we think about when we hear the word radical. We think of those sorts of things. But that's not what the word radical means. The word radical comes from the same word that we get the word "radish"

61

from. Now personally I don't eat them, but I'm told there are people who do eat them and what you're eating is the root of the plant. The word radical means "rooted in, going back to one's roots." And when I heard that young lawyer use the word that Christianity is a radicalized part of the Jewish faith I thought, he's got it. He understands a point that we often miss. We seem to forget that we as Christians didn't suddenly invent ourselves 2,000 years ago. We are rooted in our Hebrew forbearers. We are rooted in their history and their traditions. We are not something that just sprung up out of nowhere; we are a radical continuation of the Hebrew faith.

So it is that it is right for us to recall the stories of our faith. The stories of our common Judeo-Christian heritage. This passage from Deuteronomy, is one of those powerful retellings of the story. What we see here is that the people were about ready to go into the promised land and God spoke to their leader Moses. The Lord their God instructed them in what they should do when they got into the promised land. God knew what we human beings are like. When things are tough and we need God's help, we're on our knees. When things are going well, we sometimes forget who is the giver of all that is good. So he knew that they would get into the promised land and probably forget all about him. He didn't want to happen. He wanted them to remember their history. He wanted them and us to recall his great deeds and actions. God wanted us to have in our hearts and in our minds all of his dealings with us, all of his faithfulness, his providence, his guidance, his protection, his direction that he has given to us throughout all these many years.

And so Moses wrote down instructions of what they were supposed to do when they got into the promised land; they were supposed to take the first fruits of what that land provided for them; the blessings that that land gave to them; they were to bring it to God and to remind themselves of the story of their heritage. "My father was a wandering Aramean, a man from Syria who God spoke to and said I want to raise a great people out of you." And he wandered into Egypt. And when he was in Egypt, his family grew and grew and grew and grew to the point where they became a threat to the Egyptian people and when threatened the Egyptian people did what many of those times did, they enslaved these foreigners who were living in their land. And they forced these foreigners to do terribly hard labor with little or no enumeration whatsoever. It was onerous work, it was backbreaking work, many died while performing the work that was given to them. They lived their lives in anxiety, questioning the very future of their existence. They cried out to the God that led them to Egypt and said "Look at where we are! Look at what's happening to us! Look at us now! You called us to be a great people and here we are slaves." God heard their plea and raised up for them a leader by the name of Moses. And Moses bickered and argued back and forth with the Pharaoh trying to make his case and plead the cause of his people. Then they had all those plagues after which the exasperated Pharaoh relented and said, "Get out of here! You guys are being a real pain to me; I want you out of here!" And so they left Egypt. God had freed them from their slavery.

They got out on the path to the Promised Land and wandered for forty years in the wilderness. I know, this is the part where all the women in the congregation are going, "if Moses just listened to his wife and got directions, they wouldn't have had to wander for forty years." But they wandered for forty years in the wilderness. But God provided for them; gave them manna, gave them all that they needed, gave them everything to sustain them, to keep them, to nourish them, to strengthen them, to give them the ability to reach the Promised Land. It was God who had brought them to that point. He didn't want them to forget who it was that cared for them, protected them, nourished them, strengthened them, and provided for them every step along the way. He knew that we had that propensity to forget who our caregiver is. We have that propensity to forget how God provides for us. And he gave them these tools this tithe, this offering, to bring before him as a sign of saying, "it's all from you O God" and to do it joyfully and to do it gratefully. He reminds them to do it with a spirit of gratitude and thanksgiving.

Now, in every marriage you have wonderful compromises, don't you? You work things out together and you try to come up with a plan to do things and so on. In our house we have this wonderful compromise plan that Debby does all the cooking, I do all the eating, no that's not it. Oh I know how it works…. she does all the cooking and I'm responsible for clearing the table, doing the dishes, washing the pots and pans. Not a bad compromise is it? And 90% of the time, okay 75% of the time I do it with great gratitude because I recognize that if I had to exist on my cooking, I would be miserable! My diet would consist of peanut butter and jelly, grilled cheese, and a packaged macaroni and cheese. Maybe I would have an occasional slice of toast and maybe a can of soup on a good day. But I do my part of the responsibilities with gratitude recognizing that she has taken such good care of me, has fed me well, and I do those tasks with love and with gratitude for her care and providence for me.

God is asking us to bring our tithes, to bring our offerings, to bring ourselves out of recognition, a grateful, joyful recognition that it is God who provides for us. It is God who cares for us. It is God who sustains us when we are wandering around seemingly aimlessly in our lives. It is God who guides us and directs us and gets us to where we ought to be. He wants us to remember that, to keep that in our hearts, to practice that spirit of gratitude and rejoicing and recognizing all that he has done for us in so many ways.

In this season of Lent, let us remember that our father was a wandering Aramean who God provided for and cared for and brought out a great people. Let us recognize in this season of Lent, the multitude, the myriad number of ways in which God cares for us and provides for us. Amen. Let's bow our heads in prayer. O God of grace and God of glory by your hand we have been fed. We stand before you as the grateful people bringing to this time and to this place ourselves offering unto you our lives as a sign of gratitude. We joyfully give you thanks for all that you have done for us in ways of great and small. We pray this in Jesus' name. Amen.

Journey with Jesus: Oxymoron

A Communion Mediation on World Communion Sunday

Lamentations 3: 19-26

October 3, 2010

Jesus used the Hebrew Scriptures, what we call the Old Testament, as a part of his teaching ministry. He was constantly using the scriptures to shed a new light on our understanding of God and our relationship with the Holy. This morning we are going to look at a passage of that Hebrew Scripture in a book that we don't like simply because of its name. But Jesus saw that there was wisdom and insight in those pages, and it would do us well as we seek to Journey with Jesus to see this wisdom that this particular passage might have for you and me. Let's see what it says.

> *"I remember my affliction and my wandering, the bitterness and the gall! I well remember them, and my soul is down is downcast within me. Yet, this I call to mind and therefore I have hope. Because of the Lord's great love we are not consumed, for his compassions never fail; they are new every morning; great is your faithfulness. I say to myself the Lord is my portion therefore I will wait for him. The Lord is good to those whose hope is in him, to the one who seeks him. It is good to wait quietly for the salvation of the Lord."*

May the Lord bless this a portion from his holy word.

I always seem to find myself getting into trouble when I choose words for titles of my sermons. And this week I chose a word which my dad would have called a fifty-cent word. And no sooner was the title of the sermon on the bulletin board out here and the one at the chapel when somebody called me and said, "What's an oxymoron?" Somebody later on, a couple of days later, asked me the same question, "What's an oxymoron?" and I said, well, what do you think it is? They answered me and said, "Well, as near as I can tell, it's a new cleaning product for idiots." I'll try and explain it. An oxymoron is something that seems to be a contradiction but really isn't. That's all it is.

As I was driving over here very early this morning, the fog was so thick I couldn't see six feet in front of me. I actually drove below the speed limit between my house and the church. That's how thick the fog was. And, of course, I'm getting this attitude thing going – it's early in the morning, it's Sunday, I want it to be a good day for everybody, I want it to be a meaningful day for everybody and as I'm driving along in the thick fog I'm going, "O yea, great, this is going to be good for everybody. It's a gray miserable day and everybody is going to be in a bad mood on me." But I wasn't quite seeing the whole picture. Behind that fog, behind that darkness that I was driving through, was the beautiful sunshine that you and I see right now. The fog was so thick around me that I lost my perspective, I lost my ability to see what the reality really was, what the whole picture was. I lost that perspective of what was actually happening. I got so caught up in that space right around me that I couldn't see beyond it. That happens in our lives a lot, doesn't it? That happens a lot to each of us if we're honest with ourselves. We get caught in those dark moments of our lives and we quickly lose perspective. We quickly lose the big picture and we begin to draw ourselves down to the occasion instead of looking up to see our way through it.

The writer of Lamentations experienced life the same way all of us do. Is there any one of us here who hasn't had their heart broken? Is there any one of us here who hasn't felt as if the whole world was against them at some point in time? Is there any one of us here who hasn't felt the weight of the world upon their shoulders and you just weren't even sure you could put your one foot in front of the other to get yourself through the day? The writer of Lamentations knew what life was all about. He experienced it with all of its darkness. He experienced it with all of its seeming hopelessness. He understood how life oftentimes feels for each and every one of us. There is no exemption from the pains of life; there is no "Get out of Life Free" card that we can play when life is hurting.

The writer of Lamentations also could see through the fog. He could see that just beyond that darkness within his life and he expresses himself so well that he uses the term gall. How descriptive is that of

66

how we feel when we feel the whole world is collapsing in on us! You know that when he uses the phrase bitterness and gall that he is talking about how when life is so troubled that your stomach is fighting against you! He's describing how our bodies react because we are just taking it all within us and we don't know how to get out of the depths. However, in spite of all of that he was feeling and experiencing the writer knew that just beyond that fog was the light of God's love. God's providence, God's mercy, God's care for each and every one of us is always there. Great is God's faithfulness. In the midst of the gall and bitterness of his experience he proclaims: Great is God's faithfulness. New every morning are the ways God shows his love for us. We, absolutely, need to keep that hope within our hearts and within our lives.

On this Sunday you and I are going to gather around this wonderful symbolic table. You and I are going to celebrate a meal together, a simple meal. A little bit of bread, a little something to drink. But what if we stop to think about what it is that we are celebrating on this World Communion Day with others all around the world? The whole Christian church in many different languages, in many different ways and many different styles is gathering around the same table as us today to do what? To do what? To celebrate the darkest hour of the earth's history, the darkest moment that the world ever saw. Remember what the gospel writer says on the very hour in which Jesus died, "a darkness came over the whole land" literally and figuratively. You and I are gathering together to remember the death of someone who is so unique, someone who was unlike anyone else, somebody who is so special that over 2,000 years later we still try to find the right words to express our love and admiration for the man. We gather around this table to remember the darkest moment of human existence but yet in the darkest moment came the brightest light. For in his death you and I were given life.

After the sermon at Broad Avenue this morning, I have to tell you this story. There's a very special young woman who worships with us at our Broad Avenue Chapel and Marie is very special. Her mental capabilities are rather limited but sometimes she sees things that the rest of us don't always capture. After the service over there, Marie came up to me and with tears in her eyes she said, "Did Jesus die for me?" And I said, "yes Marie he died for you so that you and he could live together forever." And her tears went away, and she got this huge smile on her face and she said, "that's good!" My friends, she gets it. She gets it – what this is all about. In the darkest moment of human history, the greatest light was shining its brightest. Amen.

Wandering Arameans: Seeking Understanding

Genesis 15: 1-12, 17-18

February 28, 2010

In this season of Lent, we are pondering some of our roots – what it means to be a people called by God and how God has sought to be in relationship with us from day one. And so we look back today to the book of beginnings, the book of Genesis in the 15th chapter and I'll read selected verses there. Genesis chapter 15:

> *After this, the word of the Lord came to Abram in a vision, "Do not be afraid, Abram, I am your shield; your very great reward. But Abram said, "O sovereign Lord, what can you give me since I remain childless and the one who will inherit my estate is Eliezer of Damascus." And Abram said, "You have given to me no children, so a servant in my household will be my heir." Then the word of the Lord came to him, "This man will not be your heir but a son coming from your own body will be your heir." God took him outside and said, "Look up at the heavens and count the stars if indeed you can count them." Then he said to him, "so shall your offspring be." Abram believed the Lord and he credited it to him as righteousness. He also said to him, "I am the Lord who brought you out of Ur of the Chaldeans, to give you this land to take possession of it." But Abram said, "O sovereign Lord, how can I know that I will gain possession of it?" So the Lord said to him, "Bring me a heifer, a goat and a ram each three years old along with a dove and a young pigeon." Abram brought all of these to him, cut them in two and arranged the halves opposite of each other. The birds, however, he did not cut in half. The birds of prey came down on the carcasses, but Abram drove them away. As the sun was setting, Abram fell into deep sleep and a thick and dreadful darkness came over him. When the sun had set and the darkness had fallen, the smoking fire pot with a blazing torch appeared and passed between the pieces. On that day the Lord made a covenant with Abram and said, "To your descendants I will give this land from the river of Egypt to the great river the Euphrates."*

May the Lord bless this a portion from his holy word.

The good news for all of you is I'm going to cut to the chase on this sermon. I'm not going to press my luck with my voice going into another coughing spell. But this is a wonderful passage that tells us some of our story. I don't want to give it short shrift. In this passage there are several things that I'd like for us to see and notice as we seek to understand our heritage. I want us to seek to understand how it is that God has sought us out, how God has sought to love us and to adopt us as his sons and daughters. So it is as we read through this, the one that jumps out at me right away is Abram's desire to understand. How is all of this going to take place? Are you going to hand down my inheritance, this blessing that you're giving to me, are you going to hand it down to this household servant, this rightful heir of mine? You see in those days the law of the land was pretty straight-forward. You didn't have wills and trusts and lawyers but there was a way that things were handled. The oldest male of the household would be the inheritor. If there were no sons, then it would pass on to the oldest male servant in the house so he's asking that question. How's this all going to work anyway? Are you going to bless me but then it has to pass down to somebody who's not even related to me? And God gives a sign and I love this part. God takes him outside, and he has him look up at the stars. God does this for two reasons. Like I said, I'm cutting to the chase today, so I'll tell you really quickly what the two reasons are. God does this because he wants Abram to look up at the stars. I realize it's hard for us to imagine what Abram saw at that time because we live in a generation where's there's so much artificial light out there. We only see a portion of the stars that would have been visible in a time such as Abram lived where there was no artificial light, maybe a campfire here or there. But on the darkness of the night, on a clear night the skies would be so bright with all of the stars that were there. So God wanted to use this as a teaching tool to get him to see a couple of things; one is you can't count the stars. You just can't. And I know there are IBM types in this congregation who are trying to analyze it in their mind, "now if you took a picture of the sky and you put it into the computer", no even if you did that you're only getting one portion of the sky at one point in time. You'd have to go all the way around world on every parameter to be able to see all the stars. It's just impossible to count them. Stars come and stars go and it's an impossible task. God wanted Abram to see that his blessings would be innumerable. Abram wouldn't even be able to count the number of sons and daughters that he would have. God wanted him to see that out of that blessing to this one man it would be a blessing to the world. For you and I are Abram's sons and daughters. We have been engrafted onto that root that was planted so many many generations ago. We have been adopted into the family of faith. We have been invited to be participants in that great conversation with God. And who can number all of those who believe? Who can number all of those who have descended from that love that God showed to Abram? And so God wanted Abram to look up at the stars in the heavens and know that his blessing wasn't for Abram alone. But the blessing was for generations to generations to generations to come and to see and to know God's love.

But there is a second reason. There was a second reason that God took him outside to show him all those stars. And that was to get Abram over his qualms because Abram was a little confused. He was well up in years as the old saying goes. His wife was well up in years as well. So he was a little confused because the days of having children were gone for him and Sarah. So how was that going to work? How would that happen? And so God took him outside not only to show him the number of descendants, not only to show how many people were going to be blessed by God but to show Abram if he can put all those stars in their rightful places, helping an elderly couple to have a baby is a walk in the park. He wanted Abram to see that he is a God who does; a God who is capable of great things. That he is a God who was able to do whatever he chose to get his message across to the people.

Now, again, cutting to the chase, you know on TV when you think the ad is almost done and then the announcer says, "Wait, there's more!", there's a third thing here that I want you to see. In that 18th verse it says, "God made a covenant with Abram on that day, that the land would be Abram's and his descendants." Well, it wasn't so much the land as it was the blessing, the relationship that God was seeking with Abram and his people that would be his family. That he would be in relationship with them; they would be his sons and daughters; they would be in kinship with him. But the interesting thing about this covenant is this: covenants are an agreement between two parties such as we have in contracts nowadays which are legally binding agreements. Covenants were really more of a handshake kind of thing where it was held together by the honor of the parties involved. But each party brought to it some element. For instance, if I made a deal with you to sell you my house, we would work on the arrangements on how you pay for it, then I would sign over the title and so on. So I would give you the title, you would give me the money and we would have a covenant between us, each party bringing to the table one part. But if you look at this covenant, this covenant that God made with Abram, it's a one-sided covenant. It's a one-sided covenant! My friends, that's how God makes covenants with us. That's how God relates to us. God does everything for us. The same way that God cut through the two halves of the sacrifices, God takes care of everything. The same way that God gave to Abram a son and then grandchildren and great-grandchildren and on down through the years. It's the same way that God gave us his son, Jesus Christ. To live, to die, to be raised again from the dead, in order to be in relationship with us. While we were sinners, the scriptures tell us, Jesus Christ came for us. It's not because of anything we do, it's not because of anything we have done, it's not because of how good we are, it's because of God's great love and mercy. He does it all for us.

You and I are the recipients of a one-sided covenant. We are the beneficiaries of our God's love that reaches out to us and does everything for us so that we can be adopted into his family of sons and daughters, brothers and sisters together. God has done it all for us and the only part of the covenant that we have to do is to recognize that gift, that overwhelming gift of his love and accept that love into our hearts and into our lives. A one-sided covenant where God does it all and we need only to accept that gift into our hearts and into our lives. Amen.

Would you pray with me? Almighty and ever-loving God your grace abounds. Your mercy overflows and while we have been such an unlovable people, you have loved us. While we have wandered far away, you have come to seek us out. O gracious Lord help us to see how much you have loved each and every one of us. That you would give of yourself in every way even to the gift of your son Jesus Christ and his death upon the cross in order that you might have us as your sons and daughters, as a people that you have chosen to love. We pray this in Jesus' name. Amen.

Preacher's note: There has been much discussion within the Christian Church as to what constitutes prophetic preaching. It is often times defined as oppositional to pastoral preaching. But I would contend that it is not the opposite but rather an element of pastoral preaching. I have included in this section a few examples of why I say this. In each situation I was trying to show an awareness of the current times. (The often-misused Karl Barth statement that we need to preach with the Bible in one hand and the newspaper in the other.) In each situation I try to take a step back, search the wisdom of the Bible and give a larger perspective that will help my congregation deal with 24-hour news cycle.

Shall the Fundamentalist Win?

Galatians 5: 1, 13-25

June 30, 2019

Nearly 100 years ago in 1922 Harry Emerson Fosdick the controversial Pastor of First Presbyterian Church of NYC and later of Riverside Presbyterian Church in NYC preached a sermon entitled, "Shall the Fundamentalists Win?" At the time the majority of denominations in the US were in fear of mutual self-destruction over the challenges modernism posed against those who became known as fundamentalists. In 1922 the name fundamentalist was ascribed to those who proposed that in order to truly be a Christian one had to subscribe to a handful of "fundamentals" of the faith. No doubt or questions were allowed.

Over the years the term fundamentalist has come to enjoy a much broader definition and use. It has devolved into a less than flattering description of those who feel that they hold the truth in their hands and therefore anyone who even slightly disagrees with them is not only wrong but absolutely rejected and excluded. A fundamentalist is anyone who draws the lines in the sand that excludes, demeans and dismisses anyone who disagrees with them.

We live in a fundamentalist age but unlike 1922 where it was only the archconservatives who took fundamentalist stances, we are besieged on both the left and the right. It comes at us from both sides. The left is every bit as fundamentalist as the right. This neo-fundamentalism is absolutely exclusion oriented. "Is you is or is you ain't?" If one doesn't answer correctly on a variety of litmus tests, then one is excluded and dismissed as not being a true follower of Jesus Christ. This Fundamentalist mentality is not something new. Litmus testing in the Church is as old as the hills. Paul in his writing to the Church in Galatia, was dealing with this very same issue. At that time, in that church, they were referred to as the Judaizers

The Judaizers were insisting that in order to be a follower of the Messiah Jesus, one had to first become a full-fledged Jew. If you weren't circumcised, that needed to happen. You had to follow all of the dietary laws of being Jewish. You had to follow all of the cleanliness laws of being Jewish. You had to follow all of the holiness laws of being Jewish. In other words if you weren't fully Jewish, you certainly weren't a Christian. You were excluded. You were dismissed. You didn't pass the litmus test.

Fundamentalism in any of its forms is based upon fear and prejudice. I have mentioned before how my hometown was predominantly Roman Catholic. The ratio was roughly 13 -1. There was a great deal fear and prejudice against the small protestant community within that small city. And I can certainly understand how that came to be. It was the protestants who owned the coal mines. It was the protestants who owned the manufacturing companies. It was the protestants who owned the banks. It was the protestants who owned the stores. I understand where their fears and prejudices came from but there were painful, nonetheless.

The fourth grade was my first full year living in Carbondale. My teacher was Miss Hyde. She took the role on the first day of school and called my name. I responded and she asked me, "Are you any relation to Reverend Starzer?" I said, "Yes. He's my Dad." She looked me square in the eye and she said, "Young man, clergy do not marry, and clergy certainly do not have children." I told my parents about this exchange in the full hope and expectation that my Dad would march into that school and demand her dismissal. My hopes were dashed when Dad said, "You can't change people's hearts with an angry word. Show her how wrong she is by being the best student in that class." I didn't think I did that because I never got above a "B" that whole year no matter how hard I tried.

Catholic versus Protestant; Democrat versus Republican; Conservative versus Liberal: in a world which loves absolutes - the only absolute that truly matters is the unconditional love of God in Jesus Christ. Paul wanted the Galatians to know that the fundamentalism of the Judaizers could only be answered with the commandment to love you neighbor as yourself. And you know that those early Christians understood the parable of the good Samaritan that Jesus taught that your neighbor was with whomever you came into contact. They also heard Jesus words that we are called to love our enemies.

The Church is called to a different standard. The Church is called to a higher standard.

- we are not called to be right but to be righteous
- we are not called to be powerful but to be servants
- we are not called to be political but to be pious
- we are not called to be violent but to be peacemakers

We don't demand love, but we can and ought always to offer love: unconditional love the same as we have received from Jesus Christ himself.

In a neo-fundamentalist world we are called to be listeners. The prophet Isaiah heard that word, "Come now, let us reason together, though your sins be like scarlet, they shall be made as white as snow." We are called to live in humility as ones who are a loved and forgiven people. We are called to reach beyond our fears and prejudices to develop relationships. We are called to love our neighbor for who they are: someone God loves enough to die for.

Let me offer you this postscript. My older brother John became a teacher in the same school district we attended in my hometown. At a faculty gathering, shortly after he started, he ran into Miss Hyde. He introduced himself and she asked the question, "Are you any relation to Stephen?" His first brotherly reaction was to say no until he found out why I was in trouble, but he did say, "Yes, he's my brother." She said, "You brother was one of the nicest students I have ever taught."

Nothing is more powerful than love.

Gentle Words for Tough Times: God's Mercy & Our Minds

Romans 12: 1-3

August 27, 2017

We continue our study this summer trying to bring some positive good words in a time and era when positive things seem to be harder to find. And we're doing this study in the book of Romans. Romans has been a great source of hope and encouragement for all of us. So now it's taking a little turn here. We need to understand again what Paul was seeking to do. So let me remind you that Paul was writing this letter to the church in Rome for two purposes: one of introducing himself and trying to make a welcome for himself so that he could get there and work with them because their congregation was so important and that city were both so important for spreading the Good News of Jesus Christ. But he was also trying to help them to understand fully and completely what the message of the Gospel of Jesus Christ was. He wanted to give them some clarity and some succinctness to the understanding of the person and work of Jesus Christ and what Christ means for us and to us; what he has done and how that impacts us. Hopefully you also remember that the church at Rome was what we would call nowadays a diverse congregation. It had people in it from all across the world because Rome was a city that drew people from every way of life and every place, because it was the center. It was the capital city that drew people from everywhere for almost every reason. But part of that dynamic, part of that diversity that they were experiencing in the church in Rome was the diversity between those who grew up from all sorts of different faiths or no faith at all.

People who were practitioners of all sorts of pagan religions which were prevalent at the time; those who practiced the state religion of worshiping the Emperor and people with all sorts of different backgrounds and religions. That diverse group made up the majority of the congregation of Rome. But there was also within the congregation of Rome a minority group of those who were born and bred in the Jewish faith. And so that caused a bit of a rub in Rome as much as it did elsewhere in the Christian church in those early decades in that first century of Christianity. The question that was raised because of this issue was first and foremost the question of what do we do with all the laws? They were in a quandary because the Jewish Christians, and rightfully so, saw Christianity as being a natural extension of the Jewish faith. They saw Christianity as being nothing more and nothing less than the fulfillment of all the prophets of the Old Testament of the Hebrew scriptures. So they saw it as a seamless flow – they saw it that if one wanted to be a follower of Jesus Christ that meant that one became Jewish. Those who weren't raised in that tradition who were now coming into the Christian faith were arguing that that doesn't make any sense. And they reminded us that 600 rules to follow – you had to do all of these things and why can't we eat pork? It's a good meal! You mean I have to give up bacon to be a Christian? This church would be empty right now if you had to give up bacon to be a Christian! But it was a rub for them.

And so Paul is trying to help them to see what it is about the law. What it is that needs to be let go and what it is that needs to be kept? And so we'll pick up now in the 10th chapter of Romans beginning with the fifth verse, verses 5 through 15 in Chapter 10. "Moses writes concerning the righteousness that comes from the law, that 'the person who does these things will live by them.' But the righteousness that comes from faith says, 'Do not say in your heart, who will ascend into heaven?' (that is to bring Christ down) or who will descend into the abyss (that is to bring Christ up from the dead.) But what does it say? The word is near you, on your lips and in your heart' (that is the word of faith that we proclaim) because if you confess with your lips that Jesus is Lord and believe in your heart that God raised him from the dead, you will be saved. For one believes with the heart and so is justified and one confesses with the mouth, and so is saved." The scripture says, "No one who believes in him will be put to shame." For there is no distinction between Jew and Greek; the same Lord is Lord of all and is generous to all who call on him. For, "Everyone who calls on the name of the Lord shall be saved." But how are they to call on one in whom they have not believed? And how are they to believe in one of whom they have not heard? And how are they to hear without someone to proclaim him? And how are they to proclaim him unless they are sent? As it is written, "How beautiful are the feet or those who those who bring good news?"

There is something about the law that we like. I know that sounds like an oxymoron to say we like the law but there is something about the law or having rules that we like and we Christians have that tendency to try and place laws and rules back into our Christian faith. We all do it, don't we? I mean, how many of you have changed your pew in the last 20 years? You have your assigned seats and I know there is one family out of place today, but I won't point them out. Because we like our rules, we like having our patterns, we like having these rules that give us a formula, that give us comfort and you know there have been those times where we have maybe overdone it within the Christian church. We come up with all sorts of rules and regulations that have absolutely nothing to do with our Christian faith. There was a little Baptist church on the other side of the river when I was in Wyalusing in Pennsylvania and I got a hold of their new membership packet (I know I shouldn't of, but I got it). In that packet was a twenty page agreement, not on the theology – that was another set of papers you had to agree to – but it was a twenty page agreement as to how you would dress and what you would do, what you wouldn't do, twenty pages detailing everything that affected your life in any way, shape or form (or so it seemed to me). Everything from the length of a dress that a woman could wear, the type of make-up, beauty stuff that you could put on and the types that you couldn't and men (and this eliminated me from ever being Baptist in that church) men could not have facial hair and could not have hair that could touch their ears (well those days are gone for me) but anyhow (I'm just lucky to have anything up there) anyhow they had all of these rules, all these things that you couldn't do (it was all negatives)! As I went through this document, I saw that you couldn't play with a deck of cards, you couldn't even play solitaire with a deck of cards! You could play Rook; they had an option in there, but you couldn't play with a regular deck of cards. You couldn't play any game that involved dice: the list was seemingly endless. And before you could become a member of that church, before you could be baptized into that church, you had to sign, and have it witnessed that you would abide by all twenty pages of those rules in that congregation.

So we have gone to the extreme in some situations, we have gone to some places that just as an outsider looking in makes no sense at all to me or to 99% of us in the Christian church. But we do like laws and Paul was trying to help them to see that the laws the Jewish people were still trying to carry on were, at that point, meaningless. They didn't serve the purpose that they once had. He quotes Moses talking about that those who follow the laws will live. And yes, at one point in time, the laws were considered to be something which gave us life, that enabled us to live in a manner that would allow us to be in relationship with God. Following the law, doing all those right things, following the Ten Commandments, following the other 590 laws that they came up with would give you a relationship with God. But now Paul says that's passé. That's useless because of what Christ has done for us! It's a matter for us to acknowledge and accept that gift so freely given. It is Jesus Christ who has fulfilled the law! He is the perfection of the law as the means for us to be in relationship with God. Our relationship with God is based upon what Christ has done for us and our acknowledgement of it, our knowing it in our hearts and in our minds and our expression of that acknowledgement, our ability to say that Jesus Christ is Lord: our ability to say that Christ has died and Christ has risen and Christ shall come again (to use that ancient liturgy of the church). The ability to have Christ in our lives has made the law useless, useless as a means of salvation; useless as a means for earning the right to be in a relationship with God. For we live now in Christ and in him alone, not in the law do we find our life, but in Christ alone we find our life.

Paul is not trying to tell us here that this means now that we live as forgiven sinners, now that we not burdened by the law to be in relationship with God, it does not mean that now we're free to do as we please. It doesn't mean that we can go and do whatever we want and say to ourselves, "it doesn't matter, God's already forgiven me for this." It doesn't give us license to live our lives in any manner or way that we desire. It doesn't give us license to say whatever we please to whomever we please or to treat anybody the way that we feel like treating them. It's not a license. It is forgiveness.

You see, Martin Luther said that there are two roles for the law, and I think this echoes what Paul is saying, and John Calvin added one more. See Martin Luther said that the law has two roles, and I'm going to do them in reverse order to what he did. He said that a purpose of the law is to organize society. You have to have a law. You have to have laws in order to live together in communities, to live together as societies. You know this! Because, personally, I think driving on the left-hand side of the road is a lot more fun and exciting than driving on the right-hand side of the road. But I won't do it because we have laws that say we all drive on the right-hand side of the road. We have laws that tell us those red signs mean we should come to a complete stop before proceeding. We have all sorts of laws that don't let us do the obvious things like stealing from one another. I mean as we pass the offering plate this morning, there is a law against you taking offering out. Just want to remind you of that law. So society itself cannot function without laws. Otherwise society would collapse into chaos and we see that, on occasions where people take themselves and put themselves above the law. We saw it in Charlottesville yesterday. It broke my heart to see what was happening there. Not abiding by the laws of society, not abiding by the laws that we have, and people were hurt, people died. We need laws to keep society on an even keel, to live together, to work together, to exist together. Law still serves that important function in society.

Luther said the primary function of the law is to convict the individual person of the sin within their lives. That the role of the law is to help us to see clearly and specifically how each of us needs to have a savior. That each of us have fallen short of being the people that God has called us to be. But each of us have those fallen parts of our lives, almost on a moment-by-moment basis or at least on a daily basis. We have those things in our lives that we leave undone that we know we should have done and those things in our lives that we have done, and we know we shouldn't have done. But it is the law, it is the law that convicts us of those sins. It is the law that drives us to our knees to acknowledge that we do need Jesus Christ to be our savior, to take our sins away from us time and time and time again. For we live as forgiven sinners but we're still sinners and the law convicts us of that as we learn and grow, we understand what God is calling us to do and to be. The law is there to guide us and direct us and bring us to our knees.

Now, John Calvin, a few years later than Martin Luther, a generation younger than Martin Luther, comes along and says those two things are right. That yes, we need law to for ordering of society, we need law for the conviction of our sins. But he said there is a third purpose for the law for us as Christians. That purpose is for us to have a guide for how to live as forgiven Christians. The law is no longer a burden upon us! The law is more than that which brings us to our knees! The law becomes for us that helping hand up off of our knees and points us in the right direction in which we ought to live our lives. The law serves for us as a means to know how to live our lives, not under the compulsion of the law, but how to live our lives in gratitude for what Christ has done for us. To live our lives in a way that shows that the chief end that we have is to love God and enjoy him forever. But how do we do that? We do that by using the law to guide us. You see, Paul was trying to reflect here upon what Christ has done for us and part of what Christ has done for us is not just his death and resurrection, and not just the promise of his return, not just the promise of our salvation, but Jesus showed us how the law ought to work. He told us that law could be summed up in these two great commandments: to love the Lord your God with your heart and mind and strength, everything that you have ought to be put into loving God and, following that, to love your neighbor as yourself.

Well how did Jesus live out those two great commandments and how did he help us to understand, what does it mean to love our neighbor? What does it mean to love others? Is it just the neighbor who is next door, the one across the street, tell me it's not the one down the block from me. But Jesus time and time and time again in so many different ways helped us to see that our neighbor is anyone. Our neighbor is everyone. Tell me Jesus you can't mean to say that my enemy is my neighbor and Jesus said, "love your enemy."

The law, as we have seen it in Jesus Christ is that which guides us in our lives together. See I don't want to dwell on what happened yesterday in Charlottesville because it's just so saddening to me. That it even transpired in the first place and how it unwound in the second place. But as Christians, as ones who are called to be followers of Jesus Christ, as ones who have been released from the burden of the law, as ones who have been convicted by the law and as ones who seek to follow the law in gratitude and desire to be like Jesus Christ, we see the law, we feel the law as it's written on our hearts and we see what happened there yesterday and everything within us says this is so wrong. That we as Christians have to find some way, some means, some ability to model, exemplify, to show others what it means to truly love our neighbor. To not look at them and see them as different but to see them as the same as we are – ones who have fallen short of being the people God has called us to be. To see each other and to love each other enough to listen to the person who may be 100% diametrically opposed to everything you believe in and in offering that ear to them that they might respond by listening to you. You see, nobody ever had their mind changed by violence. Minds have been changed by love and grace and kindness. That's how Jesus exemplified it for us. That's how we ought to be living our lives. That's the example that we need to set and that's the word we need to speak when our world seems to be going in a different direction.

We, as the Christian church, need to say, "Wait! There's a better way! There's a more excellent way! Let me show you the way of love. Love of neighbor, love of God, a selfless love that just might make this world a better place." Anger, hatred, violence, they just spiral downward. But love has that ability to build up. That's what Paul is trying to help us to see. It's not about following 600 rules and judging the other person you know because they only got 598 right. It's about following the law of love. We use the law to help us to see how it is that we can be ambassadors of Christ's love in this world, sharing Christ's love through our words, through our actions, through the way we treat one another, through our ability to listen even when what we hear is repulsive to us, but that listening just maybe will give us an opportunity to speak a word of love. Our anger, our words of hatred will never open up any doors of conversation. We are called to be followers of Jesus Christ. To live not under the weight of the law, not under the compulsion of the law but to live in the spirit of the love that the law reveals to us and how we ought to live our lives day in and day out.

Would you pray with me? O God of grace and God of glory, we can never repay you for the gifts so freely given to us – the gift of your love in your Son, Jesus Christ. But what we can do, O Lord, is try to follow that example, to make that example the law that is written upon our hearts so that we live as your people, sharing your love in a world filled with anger and hatred. That we exemplify the depth and the breath and the height of your love for every person that you desire for everyone to know that love and to experience what it means to be your sons and daughters. We pray this in Jesus' name, Amen.

To See by Not Seeing

John 20: 1-8

March 27, 2016

You know you all can be honest with me; I know that you only come to hear the music. I can handle it. I can deal with the truth. The music is always the highlight of my Easter. But we do have a story to tell, don't we on this Easter Day? A story found in the 20th chapter of John, the first 18 verses there. A story I know we have heard time and time and time again, but a story that we need to hear over and over again. And so let us listen to this story that John shares with all of us on this Easter morning.

"Early on the first day of the week, while it was still dark, Mary Magdalene went to the tomb and saw that the stone had been removed from the entrance. So she came running to Simon Peter and the other disciple, the one Jesus loved, and said to them, "They have taken the Lord out of the tomb, and we don't know where they have put him" So Peter and the other disciple started for the tomb. Both were running, but the other disciple outran Peter and reached the tomb first. He bent over and looked in at the strips of linen lying there but did not go in. Then Simon Peter who was behind him arrived came following him and went straight into the tomb. He saw the strips of linen lying there, as well as the burial cloth that had been around Jesus' head. The cloth was still lying in its place, separate from the linen. Finally the other disciple, who reached the tomb first, also went inside. He saw and believed. (Though they still did not understand from scripture that Jesus had to rise from the dead.) Then the disciples went back to their homes, but Mary stood outside the tomb crying. As she wept, she bent over to look into the tomb and saw two angels in white, seated where Jesus' body had been, one at the head, the other at the foot. He asked her, 'Woman, why are you crying?' 'They have taken my Lord away,' she said, 'and I don't know where they have put him.' At this she turned around and saw Jesus standing there but did not realize it was Jesus. 'Woman,' he said, 'why are you crying? Who is it that you are looking for?' Thinking he was the gardener, she said, 'Sir if you have carried him away tell me where you have put him, and I will get him.' Jesus said to her, 'Mary.' She turned toward him and cried out in Aramaic, 'Rabboni!' (which means 'Teacher'). Jesus said, 'Do not hold on to me, for I have not yet ascended to the Father. Go instead to my brothers and tell them, 'I am returning to my Father and your Father, to my God and your God.' Mary Magdalene went to the disciples with the news: 'I have seen the Lord!' And she told them that he had said these things to her." May the Lord bless this a portion from his holy word.

We have this problem. We generally think of Easter along the line of this is something do; this is something we hear, and it is a tradition we have. We make sure to get to church; we hear the story over and over again and time and time again and we let it go in one ear and out the other ear until the next year comes and we go through it all over again. That's one of the things that we do. The other is we have this tendency to over analyze Easter. It may be that we look at it a little bit too closely and we want to see every tiny little bit of it and the smallest detail of it. Then we try to figure it all out and get every little detail down and we consider ourselves junior theologians in trying to get it all squared away. But I think that what we need to do is see it for what it is. You see John was not a historian. It wasn't about this, this, this and this - you know the way the historians do. It is instead John telling us a story. And sometimes the power of a story is its ability to touch our hearts and our lives. I think this is a story that calls for us just to listen to it, to hear it, and to enjoy it.

Sometimes when we over-analyze we miss the fun of the story and this is a story with some fun in it. And this is a story which has a lot of humanity in it and we shouldn't rush so quickly to the miraculous that we miss the ordinary. There is some wonderful ordinariness in this story. I mean you start off with Mary Magdalene probably if you did family ranking you would have to guess that she is obviously is an oldest sister. She is the responsible member of the family. Every family has that responsible member: the one who makes sure everything is done right and follows every little family tradition and makes the phone calls, makes sure that everybody is there when and where they need to be. The oldest sister generally takes that role in most families. Well, Mary is that oldest sister, right? (I'm getting a smile and a head nod from the front row, I like that! The oldest sister up here is going yep, yep! Don't worry the youngest sister gets her due in a minute so you can relax.) See it's very human isn't it? It's such a human story because Mary is the one who knows that Jesus' body wasn't properly prepared because there wasn't enough time before the Sabbath started. So she is the one who is rushing before everyone else to be there right at sunrise in order to take care of Jesus' body in a proper and decent manner. She is the responsible one. She is going to the grave to make sure things are done properly, decently and in order. Probably the first Presbyterian – decently and in order.

But then you have Peter and you have John. I like John (here's where the youngest comes in.) John was obviously a youngest brother because the youngest (now I might be a little prejudiced being the youngest of 4) but the youngest is always the favorite one. Is that not right? The youngest is always the favorite child. That is absolutely true. I know I was the favorite child in my household and John probably must have been the youngest in his family because he doesn't even refer to himself. He says John the one that Jesus loved, Jesus' favorite disciple. Now are you beginning to see the humanness of this story, aren't you? You can see this picture developing and John wants us to get into this experience and maybe even see ourselves there in that first Easter morning picturing ourselves.

In any family there are occasionally rivalries. Are there occasionally rivalries in your family? (I love having three sisters sitting together in the front row. You guys are helping me with my sermon so much today. You do realize you have to stay for the 11:00 service too.) In every family there are those sibling rivalries. Among the disciples there's this kind of sibling rivalry going on. We see that because for example, you know, on the one hand, you have Peter who is the one who gets the attention called to him all the time. Have you ever noticed that if you're reading through the Gospels it's Peter who is always is the one that's the center of attention? And then you have John who we already know was the youngest son the beloved disciple and you can tell there's some rivalry going on between them because when Mary comes to tell them the tomb is empty, who are the two that go running? It's Peter and John and the fact is that they didn't walk to get there, they ran to get there. You and I don't think it's because the tomb would be any less empty if they didn't get there in a hurry, there was a rivalry going on.

I remember when I was in the fire company in Wyalusing. It was a volunteer fire company and what we did was when there's a fire the siren would go off and everybody would go running to the fire hall. The unwritten rule was that the first one to get there had the opportunity to drive the first due engine. That was always like a position of honor. Well, we had these two young volunteer firefighters, "Bobby" and "Gary" who were always rivals with each other and would always rush to see who could get there to drive the engine. And one day I got there for a reported structure fire, I was third one to arrive at the fire hall and "Gary" and "Bobby" were standing there next to the driver's door of the engine yelling at each other arguing which one got there first. And so my buddy, Vaughn Glover arrived shortly after me. Vaughn and I looked at them and looked at each other. We knew what to do. I hopped into the driver's seat and Vaughn hopped into passenger's seat and we took the engine while the other two stood there arguing over who was going to drive.

You understand the nature of rivalries, don't you? You have these rivalries; we all have these little rivalries whether it's in the family or in the workplace or wherever it might be, and those rivalries just appear at a moment's notice and that's was what happened on that Easter morning. Mary comes back, tells them the story the tomb is empty, she didn't fully understand what she just experienced. She really wasn't sure what to do next. She was counting on Peter and John to help he figure all of this out. I don't know that they knew what was happening, so the two of them go running there and of course John (since it's his gospel) puts in the fact that he won the race. But Peter was the braver of the two and he goes in to check it out.

Now, the story is so good because you have these two guys, they've gone to check it all out. They see that the linens are lying there but there's no body! What has happened to Jesus? The linens are still there but he's not! And poor ever so responsible Mary is still very upset because she has a job to do. Don't you love that part of this? Mary, the responsible child, still has a job to do and she can't figure out how to get it done. She looks into the tomb one more time, this time she sees a couple of angels. The angels explain to her what's happening, she steps back out and she sees Jesus. But she doesn't recognize Jesus. She thinks he's the gardener, an honest mistake. Her eyes were probably clouded over from crying. She is obviously upset at the death of one upon whom she had pinned all of her hopes. The last person in the world she thought she would see standing there by the tomb that Sunday morning was the one she saw dying such a painful and disgraceful death. Being so upset, she sees Jesus there and what does she say? "Can you tell me where they've taken him? I have a job to do. I've got to take care of him. His body isn't properly prepared for burial. Can you just tell me where he is?" And Jesus calls her by name. Isn't that a touching moment as you read this story? He speaks her name and she recognizes him in the voice that he speaks her name and suddenly she knows it's Jesus.

You know we get caught up in the miraculous nature of this event. And we think of it as something that is so different from our own experiences. This is something that happened 2,000 years ago, way back when, way over in some distant land that we only know from pictures that we've seen or descriptions that we've heard. But John wants us to see this story with you and I right there in it. He wants us to step in because the disciples didn't quite get it all right. Don't you love that part where John makes note that they looked in and they saw that he was gone, and they believed but they still didn't get it? He puts that in there confessing their failure to comprehend what was happening. They still did not understand it and Mary with her inability to see Jesus when he's standing right there. You see, I think John knew. I think John understood that this is such an amazing story, such an amazing incident, such a different situation that it would be hard for us to let it all soak in. And if it took Mary who saw Jesus right there, it took her a while to hear his voice calling to her, how long will it take us? If it took Peter and John who saw the linens lying there quite a while to put two and two together, then why do we expect that we should get it all in our minds and in our heads what the full relevance is for that empty tomb for us in our lives? It takes time. It takes time. That's why we need to hear it over and over and over and over again. So that little by little by little it starts to sink into our hearts and into our lives and we start to let it dawn on us that Jesus is alive. Death has been conquered for us. That's a lot to take in. That's a lot to consider. But that's why we celebrate Easter every year so that we can hear it and rehear it until it touches the deepest part of our hearts.

Will you pray with me? O God of grace and God of glory, we confess that we are a lot like those first disciples on that first Easter morning that we see but sometimes we just don't see. We ask, O Lord, in the rehearing of the story, the retelling of the story that our eyes might be open, that we might begin to see and comprehend the fullness of the meaning and truth of the resurrection so that we might hear Jesus' voice calling each of us by our names. Help us to respond to that call with our very lives. We pray this in Jesus' name and for his sake, Amen.

God on the Move: God Moves…into the Desert

Luke 4: 1-13

March 10, 2019

Here it is, the season of Lent is upon us. Can you believe it? Here is it already!

At least for those of us who are in the ministry, it always seems to come so quickly upon us. And Lent is a very special season in the year for us as Christians. It begins with, obviously, Ash Wednesday and consists of the 40 days between Ash Wednesday and Easter Sunday. It gives us a period of time to recollect, to ponder, to consider, to share the discipline of preparing our hearts and our minds, as fully as we are able, to understand the meaning of Christ's Passion during Holy Week and the full joy and beauty of Easter – the message of Christ's resurrection. So Lent serves a very important role for us over the years. It means different things to different people, depending upon your traditions. For many people, it's a time of self-sacrifice when you give up certain things. You might give up candy bars or soda or ice-cream or something in your life you enjoy but you are willing to give up as self-discipline. That hasn't been a big thing for the Protestants overall. Over the course of the years we actually tend to the opposite. I shouldn't admit this, ever since I was a little kid growing up in a predominately Catholic town, there was nothing that tasted better than a cheeseburger on a Friday night during Lent. Just the facts.

But it is such an important time for us, and it is good for us to step back and take advantage of it. The tradition of the forty days of Lent is a tradition that takes us back to the story we're going to read from the Gospel of Luke in just a moment or two. It is taken from the journey that Jesus made in the wilderness. Those forty days where he struggled. Those forty days where he ignored temptation. Those forty days where he endured a great deal. And so it is that we pick up the theme of forty days. Possibly a reflection as well of the forty years of wandering in the wilderness for the Jewish people. It is an important number and so we, in the Christian tradition, pick that up and we take that number as our own. And now, that's what we do to commemorate Lent: forty days. But please don't go home, pull out your calendars and calculate that it starts Ash Wednesday and by Easter Day it's more than 40 days. It's 45 or 46 days, I think. Sundays don't count as part of Lent because every Sunday is, in the Christian tradition, the day of resurrection. So you can't do Lent and celebrate the day of resurrection at the same time. That's why historically the forty days is Monday through Saturday and Sundays don't count.

So if you are giving up something for Lent, if that is your desire, you get to pig out on Sunday or enjoy whatever it is that you can't do the other forty days because it doesn't count on Sundays. That's why we call it the first Sunday in Lent; not the first Sunday of Lent, it's the first Sunday in Lent. Okay, are you fully bored by now? I know there are any number of you who get bored when I turn to teaching! And on top of that it's the Sunday we set our clocks forward and I'm already fighting your tiredness! (Just for the record I did ask our head usher to take down all the license plate numbers of everyone driving in after quarter to 12 today. We'll follow up with them to remind them that they missed the services so they can go back out again.)

But this story, let me just share it with you because there is so much in here that we need to hear and to understand. It will help us to begin our Lent with understanding and meaningful preparation. In the fourth chapter of the Gospel according to Luke, we find these words:

> *Jesus, full of the Holy Spirit, returned from the Jordan was led by the Spirit into the wilderness, where for forty days he was tempted by the devil. He ate nothing at all during those days and when they were over, he was famished. The devil said to him, "if you are the Son of God, command this stone to become a loaf of bread." Jesus answered him, "It is written, 'One does not live by bread alone.'" Then the devil led him up and showed him in an instant all the kingdoms of the world. And the devil said to him, "to you I will give their glory and all this authority for it has been given over to me, and I will give it to anyone I please. If you, then, will worship me, it will all be yours." Jesus*

92

answered him, "It is written, 'Worship the Lord your God, and serve him only.'" Then the devil took him to Jerusalem and placed him on the pinnacle of the temple, saying to him, "if you are the son of God, throw yourself down from here for it is written 'He will command his angels concerning you, to protect you,' and 'On their hands they will bear you up, so you will not dash your foot against a stone.'" Jesus answered him, "It is said, 'Do not put the Lord your God to the test.'" When the devil had finished every test, he departed from him until an opportune time.

May the Lord bless this a portion from his holy word.

Under the category of "Steve needs to get a life" is the fact that I enjoy learning about what other people are preaching. It used to be you had to buy books or subscribe to a CD service where they would send you sermons on a CD and I would listen to them in my car. It always fascinates me to see what people in other churches are doing. What they're preaching on? What are their sermon series? What might their emphasis be? You can learn from others. Hopefully, it is a helpful tool to learn what others are doing and how they are doing it. So I do go online every now and then and do some research to see what other churches might be doing. Over the course of the years I've noticed a number of patterns and those patterns have changed over time. It's interesting, because it's very different now from what it was when I started out in ministry 30 some odd years ago. Basically, if a church is not following the Christian calendar, it could be an independent church, it could be a church of a denomination that doesn't hold to the Christian calendar, if that's the case, there appears to be two different patterns of how the preaching ministry goes. The first pattern is a little bit more traditional. It is that category that might fall into that of fire and brimstone which was recommended to me to do today to keep you all awake because of the time change but I opted not to do that. But it is a style of preaching that always demands a decision. At the end of the sermon it is a question of "is you is or is you not?" Are you a follower of Jesus Christ or are you not?

Well that's a good preaching style and there is nothing invalid about it at all. It is an important question to ask and it is a question that we need to ask in our hearts and our minds almost on a daily basis.

Who is it that I am following? Who is the Lord of my life? Who is it that I trust? That style of preaching is a valid style and it would really work well with this passage that we have before us today. It would fit in perfectly with that because it is where Jesus is faced with that kind of questions. Whom are you going to serve? Do you want to serve the Devil – I'll give you the whole world if you bow down and worship me. And Jesus had to decide. Do I follow the will of my Father or do I grab the glory – go with what would feel really good. This would preach well in that old school evangelistic style of preaching because it is a text that demands a verdict. It is a text that demands us to make that decision. Whom do we choose to serve? Our own self-interest or the will of our heavenly Father?

But I've noticed there is a second style of preaching that seems to be taking hold and has become a wildly popular kind of preaching. And that is what I call the self-help category. This category helps people to live their lives day in and day out within the Christian faith. For instance, one of our local churches just finished up a five-week series of sermons on Five Steps to a Happy Marriage. They carried them through all these scripture verses and helped the husbands and wives to be able to find the means and the manner to have a wonderful marriage. Well there's all sorts of categories. I've seen them on how to handle finances. I've seen them on how to have relationships with difficult neighbors. I've seen them on all sorts of categories. It's a style of preaching that is very pragmatic and helps people to do the day-to-day living in the light of the scriptures. And again, this passage would make a wonderful sermon in that category because you can see very easily and very thoroughly how easy it would be to take this story out of Jesus' life and transplant it into our lives. I could see it being a three-part series on the means and methods for dealing with temptation in our lives. And you can see that Jesus would give us some good rules of thumb for how to deal with temptations that befall us in our day to day living. I mean just see how easy it is to use the scriptures as the yardstick by which we measure whether or not something is right, or something is wrong. And Jesus had that ability when he said, "for it is written that man shall not live by bread alone. It is written that though shall not test the Lord your God." And so that would make a good sermon and I see that working in a three part series on how to deal with temptation in our lives and this story could be the basis for that and probably in many churches today the First Sunday in Lent that might be the avenue some very fine preachers will be taking with this text.

But here's the problem. If all that we see in this story, in this incident out of Jesus' life, is simply just a question of do we follow God or do we not? Or if all that we see in it is a how-to guide for us to improve our lives and to improve our decision making, then we've missed something very important today. We have missed the depth of the meaning of Christ's forty days in the wilderness. Picture yourself in that situation. Forty days, and the first thing that struck me was forty days without eating. It really might do me some good. Not sure my doctor would appreciate me going forty days without eating. Yet, I might get some good health benefits out of it. But the fact of the matter is I can't go forty minutes without eating and Debby will tell you that if I don't eat on a regular basis, I'm not fun to be around. Just yesterday we took a little day trip up to Northern Virginia. We met Courtney and her husband in Alexandria where they are going to be moving next month. My beautiful and wise wife, knowing it was going to be an hour and 45-minute trip at least, packed healthy snacks for me because she didn't want to be stranded in a car with me if I get "hangry". Just the facts ma'am. Just the facts. Forty days in the wilderness. Just not eating for 40 days and what that would do to a person. The suffering, the pain, the way the stomach reacts when it doesn't have any food going into it after even maybe 24 or 36 hours – it's downright painful to not eat anything for an extended period of time. The loneliness – can you imagine going 40 days, I know people who can't go 40 minutes without their cell phone in their hands. Forty days? Without talking to anybody? Can you imagine? I can't imagine that I could – I get lonely in the house after a couple of hours. The first hour is kind of fun by myself but after about an hour and a half I don't know what to do by myself. Forty days without human contact? Forty days of sleeping who knows where. No comfortable bed? No roof over your head? Forty days of Jesus being in the wilderness with all that he had to endure! Forty days and this right at the very start of his ministry. Forty days of having time to think about what might lie ahead. Forty days of wondering what it's all about. Forty days of questioning who you are and what you're called to do? Forty days thinking ahead to what Jesus knew would be the inevitable end. Forty days! - I can't even begin imagine what Jesus went through in his heart and in his mind throughout those forty days. It was no wonder that the devil threw temptation after temptation at him. Anyone would know that Jesus had to be at the weakest point of his life thus far. You see if all you see in this passage is an evangelistic question or a how to answer, then we have missed the meaning of this passage all together. Because what we see here is one who has experienced suffering and pain, heartache, loneliness, discouragement, whatever it may be, he has fully experienced it in those forty days! He has experienced what it means to be fully human. The fact is, that in this story, in this passage, Jesus experiences in his heart and in his life the pain, suffering, the sorrow, the concerns that you and I deal with in our lives. As the old gospel hymn says, "take it to the Lord in prayer." Because what Christ has experienced, we know that the one with whom we lift our prayers to, understands fully and completely the sorrows, the pain, the concern, the worries, the cares that we are lifting before him. The fact of the matter is everything that we might ever possibly go through, Jesus Christ has been there and done that and has the scars to prove it. The one we call our Lord and Savior, the one to whom we turn to in times of trials in our lives, has been there and done that and understands what we are going through. Now that's good news worth thinking about in our season of Lent.

Would you pray with me? Our heavenly Father, we give you thanks for the gift of your son Jesus Christ and though he held equality with you did not consider that equality something to be clung to but gave it up to become fully human experiencing the pain, the sorrow, the cares and worries of this human existence. We thank you O Lord that in him we have an advocate who truly, truly, understands what it is that we lift before you in prayer. O heavenly Father we thank you for the gift of your son, Jesus Christ through whom we are able to pray this day and every day. Amen.

Hope Realized

John 20: 1-8

April 5, 2015

We have a story, a story that needs to be told. A story that needs to be heard and reheard and heard again. A story that's recorded for us in the pages of Holy Scripture. A story that is told to us by the apostle John in the 20th chapter.

"Early on the first day of the week, while it was still dark, Mary Magdalene went to the tomb and saw that the stone had been removed from the entrance. So she came running to Simon Peter and the other disciple, the one Jesus loved, and said to them, "They have taken the Lord out of the tomb, and we don't know where they have put him" Peter and the other disciple started for the tomb. Both were running, but the other disciple outran Peter and reached the tomb first. He bent over and looked in at the strips of linen lying there but did not go in. Then Simon Peter who was behind him arrived and went into the tomb. He saw the strips of linen lying there, as well as the burial cloth that had been around Jesus' head. The cloth was folded up by itself separate from the linen. Finally the other disciple, who reached the tomb first, also went inside. He saw and believed. (Though they still did not understand from scripture that Jesus had to rise from the dead.) Then the disciples went back to their homes, but Mary stood outside the tomb crying. As she wept, she bent over to look into the tomb and saw two angels in white, seated where Jesus' body had been, one at the head, the other at the foot. They asked her, 'Woman, why are you crying?' 'They have taken my Lord away,' she said, 'and I don't know where they have put him.' At this she turned around and saw Jesus standing there but did not realize it was Jesus. 'Woman,' he said, 'why are you crying? Who is it that you are looking for?' Thinking he was the gardener, she said, 'Sir if you have carried him away tell me where you have put him, and I will get him.' Jesus said to her, 'Mary.' She turned toward him and cried out in Aramaic, 'Rabboni!' (which means 'Teacher'). Jesus said, 'Do not hold on to me, for I have not yet returned to the Father. Go instead to my brothers and tell them,

'I am returning to my Father and your Father, to my God and your God.' Mary Magdalene went to the disciples with the news: 'I have seen the Lord!' And she told them that he had said these things to her." May the Lord bless this a portion from his holy word.

Now I'm probably the only person in this room who didn't know this. I didn't realize this until I was getting ready for this sermon today but John switches tenses in the 20th chapter and without explanation he changes to the historical present tense – you all probably knew that, didn't you? Well, maybe I wasn't the only one who didn't realize that. He switches tenses here and he goes to the historical present tense. That doesn't mean anything for us in the English language because we don't have a historical present tense. But it is a tense that they used in the Greek that intends to set things apart. The only rough equivalent we have in English is when we are talking about something that is absolutely absurd we use the wrong tense such as "I wish I were the king of England," using the "were" instead of "was" because it's so outrageous it's not possible so we use the wrong tense. Well that's what this is in its use of the wrong tense. It's using something that has happened in the past but is speaking of it in the present tense. The reason that they do that is to say that this is something that has historical implications. This is something that we need to think about not as over and done but we need to think about it happening in the present tense.

As you know, a part of our Easter tradition is when we use that wonderful phrase, "He is risen, he is risen indeed." We don't say he was risen, or he has risen we say he is risen. That's our way of saying the historical present. And so it is an event that has happened, but it is an event that needs to be re-experienced and re-known and to see it in fresh eyes as if it happened this very morning. And we need to respond to that Good News as if we were the first disciples to hear that word being told to us.

I read an interesting article not too long ago and in this article this fellow was giving the reasons why he doesn't believe in the Christian faith. One of the reasons he gave was "I don't believe in the resurrection because if it were true Christians would be shouting it from the rooftops." At first, I thought, you know, he makes a good point there. It is such an astounding message: the resurrection of

Jesus Christ, that it seems as if we ought to be climbing up to the rooftops and shouting it out. But, on the other hand, sometimes good news is so deep that we have to allow it to sink into our minds and our hearts. We have to allow it the opportunity to kind of settle in and to ponder it and to think about its implications. I mean, if I won the lottery (which I can't so since I don't buy lottery tickets), but if I were to win (see there's that use of English again) the lottery, I don't think the first thing I would do is be shouting from the rooftop. I would check those numbers again and I would check those numbers again and then I would check those numbers again and I would go on the website and make sure I had the right numbers and the newspaper didn't have them wrong and I would check them all over again then maybe after I was convinced it was the right numbers I might give Gene Rosen a call and say "Gene, what will I do with all this money?" And I would get advice and I would get insight; I'd try and figure it all out and I'd be trying to fathom what it all means and trying to take it all in. That's the way it is with the resurrection of Jesus Christ. We have to listen to it and think about it over and over again. We would have to talk to others about it just to make sure we are getting it right. Maybe that is why we celebrate Easter every year without fail. Maybe that is why we always clear our calendars to be together with each other on Easter morning to hear the story again together.

There's a young woman I know by the name of Megan Bush. She is somebody I deeply admire and respect. I got a message from Megan just a week or two ago. And you have to know this about Megan, she has been through a lot in her life. Her husband is a wounded combat veteran and is a paraplegic, her son died as a toddler from a terrible accidental death. In the emptiness of their lives they decided they had too much love and they wanted to share that love. They decided to adopt a hard to place child from Haiti. They were introduced to an older child who had terrible medical problems. In all likelihood she was never going to be adopted. But Dan and Megan adopted her. Sadly, her medical conditions caught up with her and she died this past year. I got this message from Megan. She wanted me to know that she was going to buy a sign, a plaque for her children. She chose this sign because it was her daughter's favorite phrase to hear in Church. And what does the plaque say? "He is Risen." Just that one simple phrase. Nothing more and nothing less.

A simple declarative statement in the present tense talking about something which happened two thousand years ago. When I read that note from Megan, I thought she gets the big picture. She sees what this story is all about. That little plaque was not exactly going to be shouting from the rooftop, but it was going to be a quiet declaration, a declaration that Jesus Christ is alive, a quiet declaration that the tomb is empty, a quiet declaration that death has been conquered for us. A declaration that we have hope.

My friends, we have won the lottery. We have won the lottery. Jesus Christ is alive. You don't have to go home and shout that from the mountaintops. You don't have to throw open the sashes and windows and shout it at every neighbor as they pass by. But, instead, let it sink in. Let it become a part of who you are and how you perceive life. Let the good news become a part of you're going out and you're coming in. Because of the resurrection of Jesus Christ, no matter what life throws at us, we have that good news and when it's all said and done life wins. No matter what we may go through, we have hope. When it's all said and done God's love conquers all. Amen.

Would you pray with me? Almighty and ever-loving God, what good news we have. It's almost unfathomable; it's almost too hard to believe. But it is your good news that your son Jesus Christ has conquered death for us so we might live with you forever and ever. O heavenly Father help us to ponder this mystery in our hearts and in our lives so we might come to see the full picture of the height and the depth and the breath of your love toward each and every one of us. We pray this in Jesus' name. Amen.

The Crying Word
Philippians 2: 5-11 & John 1: 1-5, 14

December 14, 1980

One of the fine people whom I have had the opportunity to meet and get to know here in Scranton is Father John Essef of the Diocese of Scranton. When I was first interviewing for the job with the Congregations in Christian Mission, Dr. Carlson shared with us a story about Father Essef which I would like to share with you today. Father Essef was a parish priest during his first assignment in a mission church (which is a nice term for a congregation in a poor neighborhood that had a lot of needs). It was a cold Christmas Eve when he had just returned to the parsonage after an afternoon of hearing confessions and preparing for the evening's masses. He was tired and had not had the chance either to finish his homily for the night or even to get a bite to eat. The phone rang shortly after he got in the door. On the other end of the line was a young woman who explained her situation and asked if some food might be available from the Church. Despite his tiredness and reluctance, he assured her he would be right over. Feeling pressured by the late hour and the fact that this was one more thing to do in a busy schedule, he set out to find some canned goods to take over to her. He took these food stuffs and searched out the address she had given him. It wasn't long before he realized that this house was in a rundown section of town. When he found it, he saw before him a ramshackle building that looked unfit for any human to live in. He stepped carefully up the steps for fear of falling through the boards. Knocking on the door, the young woman answered and invited him inside. The interior was a single barren room with just a few worn pieces of furniture. Father Essef was wearing a new cassock, so he looked carefully around for a clean place to sit. As he was looking, he noticed in the middle of the floor a baby lying in an old milk crate. Suddenly his problems didn't seem so large anymore. That evening he told his congregation he had seen the Christ-Child.

And God became human, being born in the form of a man like other men. I don't think we really consider this fact at Christmas time.

Do you realize Jesus' birth was so humble that the Apostle Paul tells us Jesus emptied himself or stripped himself of all glory? I would think that being born in human form would be humbling enough: taking on the vulnerability and helplessness of a baby. But Jesus was totally emptied – no honor, no glory, no wealth, no power. God became flesh and was totally reliant upon others.

Infants are amazing. I was visiting a friend the other day and he was showing off his newborn child. His son was a fine-looking baby. Tiny little hands and feet: all his features looked so small. He was gurgling as if he were trying to say something to his father. As I was looking at the little baby, I realized how vulnerable and helpless he was. He was not able to take care of any of his own needs. He could not even say what his needs were. He was totally helpless. The best he could do would be to start crying and hope that his mother or father would soon figure out what was wrong. Babies are helpless. And God became helpless for our sakes. The miracle which we celebrate as Christmas is the fact that God became human in Jesus of Nazareth. And the greatness of this event is in the humility of the birth. God could have chosen any way to come and dwell among us. God could have chosen any situation, yet he chose the humble birth in a stable. Christ through his birth has given meaning to human life, he has given meaning to your life and to mine.

Many people today question whether life has any meaning. We read books by authors who give little value to the human life. Famous philosophers and intellectuals tell us that there is no reason for our being on this earth. When I was in college, I saw a play entitled, "Waiting for God" by Samuel Beckett. While the play was very intriguing, I was baffled by its meaning, so I asked a friend of mine what the play was supposed to be saying to the viewer. He told me that the play was not supposed to be saying anything except the fact that life is absurd. There is a segment of contemporary plays that fall under the category of theater of the absurd. For their authors life has no meaning – life is absurd.

Yet, it is not only the authors and thinkers of our time who feel that there is no rhyme or reason to our existence. It is also people who are just like you and me. This is a day and age when people are hiding more and more in the anonymity of the television set. It is as if we are saying, "Hey I don't like this world in which I am living, let me hide in the artificial world of the television." In my work this year at a prison and an alcohol detoxification center, I have seen the results of those who sought to escape from the meaninglessness of their lives through the use of alcohol or drugs. And it always breaks my heart when I read or hear about someone whose life is meaningless that they wasted it through suicide. Ours is a day and age when names are being replaced by numbers. Personal contact is replaced by mass communication. Craftsmanship and pride in our work is being replaced by mass production and higher productivity. Some say that the world is rapidly becoming de-humanized. Despair and meaninglessness are becoming the watchwords of our day.

The reason we celebrate the advent of Jesus Christ is because God has broken into the world for our sakes. Jesus' birth is the first step of God's love for us. God has come into the world not as a conquering hero but as a humble and vulnerable baby. The JOY of the Christmas season is this: God, through Jesus of Nazareth, has given meaning to the whole of our lives. [If our lives are valuable enough for God to become human, then whose is it that can say that the human life has no meaning?!!! In a world which puts greatness up on a pedestal it is ironic that meaning has come into our lives through the common event of a child being born. The world worships greatness and God has entered the world in humility – the humility of a baby. What meaning do our lives have for us?] God attached so much meaning for our lives that he gave of himself for us in Jesus of Nazareth – the Christ. God emptied himself – even to the point of being born a vulnerable little baby in a dirty stable.

Yet as humble as his birth was, the truth is that this was only a sign of the depths to which God's love would go for us. The scripture lesson tells us Jesus not only emptied himself by becoming human, he humbled himself even to the point of suffering a humiliating death upon the cross. We cannot separate the Christ-child of Bethlehem from the Crucified Christ of Jerusalem because these two events are the breadth of God's love for us. [There would seem to be no limit to the lengths that God would go for us.]

For a brief period of time I worked the 11 p.m. – 7 a.m. shift at the Treadway Inn at Princeton, New Jersey and it never ceased to amaze me how absolutely quiet it was during those small hours of the night. The silence of the night was only occasionally broken by the heating fan turning on or the sound of a truck whizzing by outside. Can you imagine how quiet it must have been nearly 2000 years ago in a rural town called Bethlehem? The anguish and despair of the world was answered during that night, not by the mighty armies of a king, not by the high-sounding words of a philosopher, not by some magical new product of a giant corporation. No, the fears, despair, and anguish of the human life was answered by God through the crying and the tears of a little baby. What meaning has life for you and me? Hope and meaning has come into the world during a silent night which was only broken by the crying of a newborn baby, "And the Word became flesh and dwelt among us…"

Let us pray,

Oh, Lord, our God and our Father,

We do praise you and worship you for being a loving and kind God.

We thank you for your Son, Jesus Christ, who dwelt with us in human form. We honor you and praise you and give you the glory as we bow down and confess that Jesus Christ is Lord. Amen.

Transfiguration
Matthew 7:1-9

February 26, 2017

Today's an in-between day. Every now and then you hit an in-between and we as Presbyterians, one of the things that we do as part of our tradition, is we try and follow the calendar of the Christian year. Many denominations do this. This is isn't something unique to us. This is really part of the whole Christian tradition and the majority of Christians throughout the world do follow the Christian calendar. And the purpose of the Christian calendar is that within the course of twelve months you will hear the whole story of the Gospel of Jesus Christ. The Christian calendar starts with the season of Advent – the preparation for the coming of Christ that goes through Christmas and so on. And we're familiar with the big days of the Christian calendar Lent and Advent, Christmas and Easter, maybe Pentecost but other than that we miss out on a lot of the smaller days on the Christian calendar. And today is one of those days. This is, on the Christian calendar, Transfiguration Sunday. Now it's not a big one; we don't all have to rush out and get our Transfiguration Sunday's dinner prepared or anything like that. This is one of those more subtle holidays but it's also on the Christian calendar one of the more confusing ones and so I'm going to attempt to preach on it. Darren was very reassuring to me this morning when I said I'm not sure it's going to make any sense when I'm done but he told me now remember the disciples were there and they didn't make any sense out of it either. So it's okay if you go home scratching your heads because it is an interesting and different experience in the life of the disciples and Jesus' life. But I think that it was important enough for our forbearers to include this as a regular part of our understanding of the story of Jesus Christ, his person and his work, his purpose in this world. So it was important enough for Matthew to include it in his Gospel; it's important enough for the Christian church to set aside a day every year, so it has a purpose, so it has a meaning for us and hopefully we'll see some of that today.

And it's found in the 17ᵗʰ chapter of the Gospel according to Matthew.

> *"After six days Jesus took with him Peter and James and John the brother of James and led them up a high mountain by themselves. There he was transfigured before them. His face shone like the sun, and his clothes became as white as the light and just then there appeared before them Moses and Elijah, talking with Jesus. Peter said to Jesus, "Lord, it is good for us to be here; if you wish, I will put up three shelters, one for you, one for Moses, and one for Elijah." While he was still speaking, a bright cloud enveloped them, and a voice from the cloud said, "This is my Son whom I love; with him I am well pleased; listen to him!" When the disciples heard this, they fell face down to the ground terrified. But Jesus came and touched them, saying, "Get up" he said. Don't be afraid." When they looked up, they saw no one except Jesus. As they were coming down from the mountain, Jesus instructed them, "don't tell anyone what you have seen until the Son of man has been raised from the dead."*

May the Lord bless this a portion from his holy word.

Even the name of the holiday is one that is a little unusual for us. It's not a word that we use in our everyday language. We don't talk about somebody being transfigured or we don't talk about this situation being transfigured. We don't use the word transfigured in our general usage of the English language. And so I thought, well, the first thing I would do is maybe try to figure out how to define it and take a look at it and understand it. It's interesting because as a preacher as you're doing this kind preparation, as you're doing this kind of study, the first thing you do is take a look back at the Greek to see what the Greek word was. And the Greek word is metamorphous. Anybody remember that from biology? I barely do. I didn't do well in biology; I'll be honest about that. The only thing that I remember about it is the word that we use to describe when a caterpillar goes into its cocoon then comes out as a butterfly. That's a metamorphous. And that's the word that the text uses in the Greek; that's the word which is translated into English as transfiguration. That it is a radical change in the being and the nature of the person. Is that helpful? Are you with me so far? I know this is a tough one. You just have to hang on a little bit with me. And so we're talking about a situation where Jesus and some of his disciples went up on the mountaintop and in the passage, Matthew doesn't tell us what the purpose was. Probably the disciples didn't know the purpose. Obviously, Jesus knew. But the disciples didn't ask. They just went along with him. Following Jesus' lead they went up to the mountaintop. While they were there this transfiguration happened to Jesus. This metamorphous of his being happened while they were on top of that mountain. Now if that wasn't odd enough, there appeared alongside Jesus, Elijah and Moses. And they were in that transfigured state as well.

Now you have to love this story because you have Peter involved. James and John – not a peep out of them. Peter, the type A personality, figures he has to say something, he's got to do something. You know he can't just sit there and be in awe of what is happening. He can't just sit there and take it all in. So he goes to Jesus and says, "You know what? It's good that we're here, we love being here with you. And if it would make it easier for you, we'll put up three shelters. I can build them right here for you." You know the type A personality that I'm talking about? Yes, that was Peter. Didn't know what was going on, didn't understand what was happening, but he knew he was supposed to do something. He knew he could build some shelters; he could build some place for them to be comfortable and stay So his idea was I don't understand what's going on, it's confusing and it's perplexing. I think I'll build something. Type A personalities – you got to be doing something. You know I'm a type C-minus personality myself. You know I'll sit there and think about it all day. It doesn't bother me. But Peter and the disciples were obviously confused as to what was happening. And everything was happening so quickly that Peter, while he is rambling on to Jesus about this situation of being there with Jesus and Moses and Elijah on top of the mountain. In the midst of his rambling at Jesus that God interrupts him. I like that part. While you're still talking, God spoke up and said, "This is my Son and I'm very, very, happy with him." Now the disciples did exactly what would be done by anyone of us: drop to the ground, hide your face and pray your heart out. You know that's what they did. And then they got brave enough after Jesus put his hand on them and said, "it's okay, it's okay." I love the reassuring Jesus. Isn't he nice? I like that about him. He's always kind and gentle. "It's alright. No need to be afraid." He puts his hand on them and tells them, "come on, let's get up" and when they arose, everything was as it was before. Moses, Elijah were gone. Jesus is himself again – the way that they knew him.

I think Darren's right. Those disciples must have been so absolutely confused at that point in time and I think that they were probably greatly relieved when Jesus said, "don't tell anybody until after the resurrection." I don't think they had any desire to try and explain what they had seen to anybody else. I think that they were happy just to have it in their lives and have it over and done with.

Well why is this such an important story for us? Why is this story worthy of our spending some time on a Sunday morning? Is it simply to figure it out and to ponder it in our hearts and in our minds? I think that one of the reasons it is so important is that it tells us about the person of Jesus Christ. We're heading now, this Wednesday, we begin our journey within Lent. It's forty days for us to look at ourselves. Forty days for us to consider what God has done for us through his son Jesus Christ. In order to understand it, we have to see who Jesus is more clearly before we can fully understand and what it is that he has done for us. This revelation, this transfiguration shows us the divinity of Jesus Christ, the one who was elevated, the one who was so different from you and I, the one that God looked at and said, "this is my son. I'm really, really, proud of him." It elevates Jesus. It helps us to see that Jesus was more than just a good teacher, an iterant preacher, traveling prophet: that he was the very son of God, living with us, dwelling with us, showing us who God is and how it is we ought to live our lives. And so, during this season of Lent, as we measure ourselves, we now have this guide by which we measure ourselves. We now have this standard to which we hold ourselves accountable in this person of Jesus Christ.

I think there is another element to it. Because I think that when Jesus told the disciples that they were not to say anything to anybody that that was very important. Now, if this was Mark's gospel, we'd be more used to that. Because in Mark it's constantly "now's not the time, now's not time, don't say anything to anybody, don't say anything to anybody", that's the constant theme running through

Mark's gospel. But for Matthew, it stands out because that is not a consistent part of how Matthew tells the gospel story. Matthew is generally one who wants to encourage others to share who Jesus is. And so for Matthew to record that Jesus said, "don't tell anybody until after I'm raised from the dead," I don't think it was letting the disciples off the hook. I don't think it was Jesus saying to the disciples, "Don't worry! You don't have to tell anybody about what you've seen here." But what it was, I think, was a gift to them to understand what was going to happen. You see, we don't always use the term "resurrection" correctly. We sometimes use the term "resurrection" when we mean resuscitation or revivication, something being brought back to life. What Jesus showed the disciples on that mountaintop was resurrection. First of all you had Moses and Elijah there who were recognizable. They were there as persons, as people, but transfigured, metamorphosed. You had Jesus transfigured into something more glorious than what you and I are. I think he wanted the disciples to see and understand that the resurrection would not be about Jesus just coming back to life but a foretaste for us, of our transfiguration in the day of our resurrection. That when he conquers death for us, he conquers it in such a way that we will be transfigured, we will be metamorphosed in our lives. We'll still be known. We'll still be knowable. We will still be who we are, but we will be the best of who we are. I think it was a gift to the disciples and certainly it was a gift to every one of us to have that glimpse of what it's all about. This one in whom God was well pleased showed us the ultimate goal, the ultimate destiny that he wants for each and every one of us. For us to be transfigured into a glorious person in the light and grace of God's love. Would you pray with me?

Almighty and ever-loving God we thank you for the gift of your son Jesus Christ who is that revelation to us of who you are and what you desire for us. Help us, O Lord, to look at his face and see in him who it is you are calling us to emulate, to become like. Help us O Lord as we seek to be followers of Jesus Christ each and every day even unto the day of our transfiguration. We pray this in Jesus name and for his sake. Amen.

Preachers Note: A Pastor's role is never more clearly defined than in the celebration of a wedding or in the remembrance of a funeral. It is also when the Pastor's heart is most clearly seen. I have included four moments in my ministry which were not only deep moments for me but also most representative of my pastoral ministry. Henri Moore was not just my supervisor in the Hanover Fire/EMS but a dear friend and brother. His death at such a young age was a tragedy for the community as well as for the department. These words were spoken at his gravesite before what very well may have been the largest gathering I will ever speak to. My brother John died of cancer shortly before his 60th birthday. The sermon included here were the words I spoke to my family and my congregation on what would have been John's 60th birthday. I included the sermon I preached at Riley Young's funeral because Riley was not only one of the quiet saints who makes a church strong but he was a dear friend with whom I enjoyed many wonderful conversations in the too few years I was able to know him. Of course weddings are always a joyful occasion for us as Pastors. They are all beautiful and meaningful each in their own way. I included the homily for my friends Lisa Bowdish and her now husband Bob Weyant because it shows the joy of a wedding between two people whose love is amplified by the love of Jesus Christ within their lives.

A Third First

Romans 14: 7-12

June 16, 1996

The title of this sermon bears some explanation. It has little or nothing to do with the sermon except for this: I have now had three first for Father's Day. My first first was when Courtney was born, and I was a Father for the first time on a Father's Day. The second first was when Chad was born, and I celebrated my first Father's Day as Chad's Dad. For each of those firsts, I wrote my sermons in letter forms to each of my kids. Today, though, marks a difficult third first for me as my first Father's Day without my Dad. In my own tradition I wrote a letter to my Dad which I would like to share with you today.

Dear Dad,

This is my first Father's Day without you. It was a year ago on Father's Day 1995 that the stroke which would finally take you from us first struck. You managed to get through the 8:30 service at Waymart and Mom wanted you to go to the hospital to find out what was wrong with you. But you refused. You did acquiesce and let John drive you to the 11:00 service at Union Dale. In spite of everything working against you, you managed to lead the worship and preach the sermon without anybody noticing that anything was wrong.

Some people attribute that action to determination or stubbornness, you can take your pick what you call it. But those of us who knew you best realize that it was simply because there was nothing in life that thrilled you more than to publicly proclaim the good news of Jesus Christ. The thought of leaving a congregation waiting to hear without a preacher available was beyond the scope of your comprehension.

It was that good news that summed up your life. Being the old school German that you were expressing your love came very hard for you. But what you had difficulty saying you had no difficulty showing. I have listened as there are those in the Church who would tell me that I should not speak of God as my heavenly Father – I understand when they tell me that there are those for whom the image of Father does not speak well – I understand and am sympathetic to that. But I can't give up the language of God as my heavenly Father because to me it speaks volumes of a relationship of love. A love that knows when to be tender and compassionate; a love that knows when to be firm and reproving; a love that knows when to say yes and a love that knows when and how to say no. I understand God's love because I understand your love. I understand God as my heavenly Father simply because you were for me a Christ-like Father.

Like Jesus, you had story for any situation. Those stories taught us well. My favorite probably will always be the one that involved you and Grandpop. It was a time when you were coming home as a youngster and were accosted by a gang of older boys. They did rough you up a bit, but you left with the threat of bringing your firefighter Father back with you. Grandpop agreed to go straighten out the situation. I can only imagine the pride you must have felt as you walked side by side with Grandpop, his broad shoulders and massive muscles strengthened from years of strenuous hard work. When Grandpop spoke to those boys you knew those ruffians would listen. I can imagine the look on your face when Grandpop said to those boys, "Give me your best man and my son will take him on."

Like Grandpop, you never fought any of our fights for us. But we always knew you were there for us and with us. It's been like that for me in ministry. You never did solve any of my problems for me, but you were always there when I needed to talk things over. Your wisdom from your experience always managed to give me a larger perspective and helped me to see things better. When I was faced with those who were disappointed with me, I was reminded of your conversation with Monsignor Horan at one of your retirement dinners. After listening to speaker after speaker praise you, Monsignor Horan turned to you and said, "Charlie, isn't there anyone in your church who doesn't like you?" To which you responded, "Sure, over 23 years there were quite a few, but I buried the last one."

Oh, by the way Dad, you will always get the blame for this odd sense of humor I have. I will always be grateful to you for teaching us all how to laugh. You taught us that everything was in God's good hands and if that was true then we should be able to laugh and enjoy life. You taught us that the worst thing in life was death, but you were quick to point out that death had been overruled by our Lord and Savior Jesus Christ. It was that perspective that helped me to deal with your final illness.

"Whether we live or whether we die we belong to Jesus Christ." (Romans 14:8b) That's all I needed to know. I know you're in a better place now. I imagine you probably look a lot like that picture I have of you when you were in your early twenties. I can guess that you've caught up with your folks and Uncle Fred as well as Uncle Al and Aunt Peggy. I can probably assume that in heaven you've learned how to sing so that John Jenkins doesn't have to go through eternity tugging on your pulpit robe to remind you to step back from the microphone during the singing of the hymns. I also know that there will come the day when we will all be together again because you showed us that the love of Jesus Christ knows no end but is eternal.

I can tell you this, Dad, not a Father's Day will go by that I won't give thanks to our heavenly Father for you. You shaped my life in the most positive ways. When people compare the two of us, I take that as the highest compliment. I only hope and pray that when my life draws to a conclusion here on earth that I will have given the full measure of devotion to our Lord Jesus Christ as you did in word and deed. I know that when Jesus greeted you, he said, *"Well done, my good and faithful servant."* (Matthew 25:23)

With all my love,

Your youngest son

Letter to Courtney
Father's Day

June 18, 1989

Dear Courtney,

Today is Father's Day. I know that doesn't mean anything to you yet. But it is a very special day to me. You see this is my first Father's Day as a Father. But that is only one of the many changes you have brought into your Mother's and my lives. You have given to us far more than we have given to you and we are glad you are here.

There is much I would like to tell you today. My heart and my mind are full of thoughts and ideas I would like to share with you. I hope God will give us time for me to share those dreams and ideas as you grow. But this being our first Father's Day together, I wanted to at least put some things down on paper for you to read when you get a little bit older and are better able to understand.

I am proud to be your Father. I love you. I happen to think that you are the most beautiful baby ever born. I am convinced that you are the most intelligent, clever, personable baby ever to crawl. You may not be, but as your father, I am allowed to be extra proud. I think there is something which is built into every Father to see the best in his son or daughter. I think it is supposed to be that way so that we can help you to reach all of the potential which lies within you. God gives each of us a variety of gifts, talents and abilities. I hope that maybe I can help you to find yours so that you can help other people find theirs.

You see God created this world where we are all brothers and sisters together. As you enjoy laughing and playing with others right now, as you grow up you will also enjoy working and talking with other people. That's how God created us. He didn't want us to be alone – he wants us to have friends and to enjoy each other. I think that is why he created the Church. I know there will be times when you will think of the Church as that place which steals your Daddy's time away from you. I know that I thought that a lot about your Grandfather Starzer. It seemed to me that he was always running off to the "Church" or to the hospital to see someone or to someone's house because they were lonely. I guess I had to be a little bit older before I realized that the Church which stole my Father's time so often gave to me more mothers and fathers and sisters and brothers and aunts and uncles and grandmothers and grandfathers as we shared in love together.

Courtney, you are a very fortunate girl. You have been born into a very warm and loving community. And God has given you the love of not one church but two. Always know that these people are your extended family. The same God who called your Daddy away from his family to this place has given us more family than we could ever hope or dream of. I will not be the perfect father to you, I will try but I cannot hope to be. But when I fail as a father or when your mother fails as your mother there are others who will be there for you. Let them love you and return their love to them. That is why God has called us to be together as His Church.

I keep mentioning God, but I haven't explained Him to you. God is the most important person in all of the world. He is the one who gave you to us. He loves you. I love you and God loves you. I am your Father here and now, but God is also your Father. There isn't anything your Heavenly Father wouldn't do for you if you really needed. He has a Son, named Jesus. God loves you so much that he gave his own son up for you. God wants to be close to you. He wants you to think of Him as your Daddy too. That's what the Bible tells us. Someday, I hope you will know this not just because I tell you but because you will have experienced his love. You can't see God, not yet at least, but you will be able to sense his presence in your life. Often times God loves us through the love of other people. Always remember that.

Courtney Anne Starzer, this is yours and my first Father's Day as Father and Daughter. I don't think I can put into words how much that means to me. Being your Father comes easily but being your Daddy will come harder. It will take a lot of hard work to be there when you need me, to provide for your physical, emotional and spiritual needs, to provide you with the discipline and guidance you will need to grow up on this world today. I will fail you, I am sure, but that doesn't mean I won't always love you. God is the one who will never fail you and God will never cease to love you.

Someday, when you are able to talk and to understand what Father's Day is, I am sure that you will wish me a Happy Father's Day. But for today, just having you here has made me very happy on this Father's Day.

With all my love,

Daddy

Dear John Charles

Father's Day

June 16, 1991

Dear John Charles,

What a name for you to have to bear. I guess that is why your Mother and I prefer to call you by your nickname of "Chad". Oh, it's not that your real name is too long or pretentious or anything like that. As a matter of fact, we are very proud of your name for you bear the names of innumerable Uncles and great-grandfathers but most importantly you carry the names of your two Grandfathers – my Dad and your Mother's Dad. With a preacher for a Dad we worried about naming you after your two preacher-grandfathers. It is too much of a burden for you to bear. Have we placed unfairly upon you too many hopes and expectations which are not rightly for us to give? We hope and pray not.

What I hope we have done is to allow you to be a part of a good and Godly heritage. Your Grand-daddy and your Grandpop are people men whom you should always admire and respect not because they are preachers but because they are good Christian men who were willing to do what God called them to do. Whether you grow up to dig ditches or teach technology, if you are doing it because it is your calling from God then you will be following in their footsteps.

I'm writing this letter to you on our first Father's Day together as Father and Son. I know it will be a few years before you will be able to read this simple letter and it will be a few years after that before you will understand what I am trying to say but I needed to say these things now nonetheless. I have been proud of you since the moment I first knew you were "to be". Yet from the moment I first laid eyes on you I was overwhelmed by the responsibility of being your Father. I wasn't worried about feeding you or keeping a roof over your head. Those things are easy compared to what concerned me.

I'm enclosing with this letter a passage of Scripture that has challenged me as I have thought about those concerns I have for your development. It's from the book of Deuteronomy – which means that law twice told – there are going to be many times, I am sure, where I will have to lay down the law more than once with you. But anyhow, there are within this passage two things which have struck me.

The writer tells the people that they are to share God's word with their children when they are standing up and sitting down and walking along the road or just about any other time of the day. That's quite a tall order, I hope I don't take that too literally and end up preaching to you night and day. I remember when I was growing up with your Uncle Paul, Uncle John, Aunt Miriam and your Grandmom and Grandpop that all six of us would sit down to the dinner table and all of the food would be out on the table and either your Grandmother or your Grandfather would pull out their Bible and their devotional guide and we would study some passage of Scripture and its meaning for our lives. You know, I don't remember a thing that we learned around the dinner table during the devotions. I do remember worrying whether the mashed potatoes were getting cold or whether that thin layer of stuff was going to form over the top of the gravy.

There will be times for us to pray and study together, but I will try to teach you the Christian faith the same way my Mom and Dad did: every day in every part of their lives. I used to travel around visiting people with your Grandpop and I saw how he held their hands and how he prayed with them. I listened as your Grandmom would talk on the telephone with someone who was lonely or afraid or discouraged. I watched your Grandpop as he never preached something that he wasn't already trying to practice.

I guess what I am saying, my son, is that I will try to teach you God's love and grace by practicing it with you. You might not always like how it takes shape because sometimes God loves us enough to say no and there will be many times when I will love you enough to say no. When I said before that it is an awesome responsibility to be your Dad that is exactly what I meant, I want you to be able to see Jesus Christ through me and I won't always live up to that goal.

I said there were two things in that Scripture passage that I wanted to share with you, didn't I? (You'll have to bear with your Dad's forgetfulness a lot in life. I hope it will teach you how to be patient and to forgive.) Anyhow, the second thing in that passage is a lesson for me, maybe more so than for you. I have to trust God. As you lie in your playpen in the living room while I am typing this, I realize how helpless you are as an infant. You need us to feed you and clean you and clothe you and to love you. That doesn't change much in going through life – I mean we do eventually learn how to feed and clothe ourselves but deep down inside we are still very helpless – we need our heavenly Father.

I will always need to remember to trust God with your ultimate care. Whatever kind of a job I do as your Father – I know that your heavenly Father is the one who truly cares for you and will always be there for you throughout your life day in and day out. When the Israelites crossed into the promised land, they were quick to forget that it was God who brought them out of the land of slavery. There will be a time when your Mom and I will have to let you go and you will feel a real sense of freedom and independence. But we will know and hopefully you will know that you still need God. God will never forget or forsake you. We trust God and we hope you will too.

I guess, John Charles, all of this is just a long roundabout way of saying I love you. I will always love you. I'm glad you are here. I'm glad you and I are able to share this Fathers' Day and I look forward too many more together.

With all my love,

Dad

Journey with Jesus: Hope & Uncle John
1 Thessalonians 4: 13-14

October 10, 2010

I hope you don't mind my doing this today but as all of you are aware, I lost my brother John to cancer just a short little while ago, so obviously in my heart and in my life is that loss that I'm feeling. And I'm blessed today because you have more Starzers in one place than any other spot in the world. There's not many of us but you got most of us here today and so welcome to my family who is here with us today to remember my brother John and all that he has meant to us and all of the wonderful memories that we have of him.

My brother John as many of knew, was the brother that looked most like me. I did not get the skinny genes that my oldest brother Paul has, I got cheated in the genetics pool. But John and I always looked enough alike that people knew that we were brothers and sometimes that was good; sometimes that was real good because John was a good student in high school, he was well behaved, he did very well in his classes and he actually graduated second in his graduating class.

And I being five years younger showed up at our hometown high school looking something like him, therefore I had immediate identification. It worked greatly in my favor because a teacher would catch me in the hallway and say, "you're a Starzer aren't you?" I'd answer, "yes I am" and they'd say "okay well I know you are alright, so go ahead and do what you're doing. Then get back to your classroom." I can proudly tell you that I went through four years at the Benjamin Franklin High School in Carbondale, PA and never once did I have to show a hall pass. So my thanks to my older siblings for paving the way for me to get away with a lot of good stuff. Especially thank you to my brother John for the privilege of looking like him that opened a lot of doors.

Sometimes having my brother John look like me could work against me at because John might not always have been as sensitive to what it means to be a pastor as I am. For instance, when I first arrived in

Wyalusing and was moving into the manse, John was nice enough to come up and help me to move in. You need to know that the manse in Wyalusing was right there on one of the main streets and had this beautiful porch on the front of the house with a nice railing on it; a great place to spend a summer afternoon. After he had worked diligently to get me moved in John decided that this would be a good time to sit and have a beer and a cigar. So he sat down on the front porch of the manse, propped his feet up on the railing, smoked a big cigar and had a bottle of Yuengling in hand and waved to everybody who went by. He knew what he was doing. He absolutely knew what he was doing. He, intentionally or unintentionally, set me up there because people in Wyalusing knew there was a new Presbyterian minister, but they couldn't tell him from me!

My brother John taught elementary school for over 35 years. He taught elementary math and it was appropriate for him to become a math teacher - he was born 10-10-50. Today would have been my brother John's 60th birthday. He taught remedial elementary mathematics or Title 1 or whatever they call it nowadays. And he taught it well over those 35 plus years in the Carbondale Area School District. In his retirement, actually even before he retired, he started to teach Math on the college level. So he went from teaching elementary math to teaching statistics at the college level which still boggles my mind since I never took statistics, never wanted to take statistics and my aversion to taking statistics kept me from being a double major with the added psychology degree. Unlike his kid brother, he enjoyed teaching elementary math and he loved teaching statistics full time on the college level when he retired from teaching in the elementary schools.

John had such diverse interests: now you figure this one out. My brother John loved Chad and Jeremy. Anyone here remember Chad and Jeremy the musicians? Yes, a few of you do. A group out of the 60's and 70's if I remember correctly. He also loved Wagnerian opera. He went from both extremes. He had such diverse interests and enjoyed so many things in life: literature and history and music. John built a lot of the furniture he had in his and Linda's house. He just enjoyed so much in life. He held such diverse interests. One of the things John loved to do was to travel, as long as it did not involve an airplane. He would travel by car or he would travel by train, but he would not travel by airplane. I know why and our brother Paul will remember why John never liked to fly. It all goes back to my high school days. I had a friend in high school by the name of Daniel Harkenreader, who was getting his private pilot's license. In order to do that, after he soloed, he would invite others along to fly with him. We'd all share the costs of the plane, so he got more hours with spending less money. I talked Paul and John into flying with Danny Harkenreader and me and as a young pilot you do make mistakes now and then. On the controls on the plane were two lever controls, one switch right next to the other. One switch was for the carburetor deicing and the other switch was for the mixture to thin it or thicken the mixture with more fuel. We were flying fairly high and Harkenreader decided he needed to turn on the deicer for the carburetor, so he reached over to do that. However, instead, he turned the fuel mixture all the way down to off. Other than flying in a glider, flying in an airplane is not supposed to be silent. As young and inexperienced as my friend was, he never panicked. He returned the mixture to it right setting and restarted the engine. Obviously, we were just fine. I have a hunch that's why John never liked to fly after that day.

But John would travel anywhere. He used to come out to see me when I was in college outside of Chicago. He'd take the train out and have a good time on the travels back and forth and we had such good times touring the city of Chicago enjoying that experience. And one of the things that John has been doing for a number of years and one of the reasons why today is also significant is every fall John and his wife Linda and our good family member Jim Burke (who we are very proud and privileged to have with us today) would travel up here to Conklin. We'd worship together and go out to eat together and we would do some touring around and we always enjoyed doing that. Last year we got to go up to Ithaca after church. We spent the afternoon there with Courtney touring the Cornell Campus. That was a great day and a deeply cherished memory.

I know there were a number of you in this congregation who were always grateful when you saw my brother John here for a worship service. You had learned that there was something going on between the two of us. You had learned that John and I had a deal we made. If I kept the sermon under 15 minutes, he would buy dinner. If it went over 15 minutes, I had to buy dinner. So Damien that's why you're doing your Uncle John's job of keeping track of the time for us today. Did you set the timer? Ok. So then if I'm under 15 minutes today, Damien is buying lunch this noon.

All of us in the family have great stories of my brother John I'm sure. More than I can share in these scant fifteen minutes! We are going to go out to dinner after the worship service today. We're going over to Niko's, which was John's favorite restaurant up here and swap some of those stories and do some of that remembering and enjoy that time together.

One of the things that was always so special, and the reason I refer to him as Uncle John is John and Linda never were blessed with children and they always treated their nephews and nieces beautifully well. Did they not? Uncle John was probably the proudest title he had. We joked with him and called him professor, we called him all sorts of titles, Mr. Starzer and so on but Uncle John was always his favorite name and he just adored all of his nephews and nieces and great nephews and nieces at this point in time and just a quietly generous person who always loved to do for others. One of the things, I'm probably the only person who knows this, is that John would always love to do things anonymously; would love to give anonymous gifts and more times than I can count he would stick significant amounts of cash in an envelope and leave it at a church that he knew needed some extra money. And when I was the go-between, he'd say, "just don't tell Linda." And so he always liked to do things anonymously and generously. As a matter of fact, one thing I will always remember is after we had the flood here, he was asking how we were doing in our house and I said "Well, we're doing good except we can't get the basement dry. There are no dehumidifiers available anywhere that we can find in Broome County. We bought them all for the flood center and they're all loaned out" and so John got into his car, ran down to Sears in Scranton and bought four dehumidifiers and drove them up for us to have and wouldn't accept a penny in return for his efforts. It was just the kind of person my brother John was and a church man as well and I need to say that between my two brothers there's not a job title in a church that one or the other of them didn't have. Between Sunday School Superintendent and Custodian, Elder,

Deacon, Trustee, everything between the two of them and John was a very loyal member of his congregation in Waymart following Dad there when Dad retired, he started to serve the Waymart church. He was just a very valued person in that congregation.

I know I'm rambling on and that's part of grieving isn't it? It's that telling of stories and remembering memories and just sometimes you just have to say them out loud so that you can hear them and cherish them and enjoy them and to keep them alive. That is a very important part of the grief process and this passage that I read from I Thessalonians today is such a crucial one for us as Christians to hear and to understand because the wisdom here is that we as Christians should grieve. It's okay to grieve. Grief is a very real and powerful thing and its okay as Christians to have that sadness in our hearts when we lose somebody who was special to us. It's okay to have that pain at losing opportunities that we would have loved to have had. I would have loved to have had my brother John here today and we'd take a ride some place and enjoy some of the scenery and all that this area has to offer.

So grief is okay. To grieve is healthy, to grieve is good and all of us, all of us, have lost or will lose somebody very special to us. None of us get through life unscathed by the pain of death. But what the Apostle Paul is trying to say to us is that it's good to grieve, it's okay to grieve, but we don't grieve in the same way as people who do not have hope. We have hope as Christians. We have that hope as I was talking with the kids earlier that there will be that day when we will be reunited with those whom we love. That day when we will be back together again with those who have gone before us and we will know them, and they will know us. And we will experience that love, we will experience that kindred fellowship that we enjoyed on earth. We have that hope as Christians that death is defeated. Death has been conquered for us by the gift of Jesus Christ in his life, death and resurrection. That death is for us as Christians just a transition from a good life to an even greater life. From something that has beauty within it to something that is eternally beautiful. We grieve, we mourn, we feel the sadness, the pain. We shed the tears when we lose people who are special to us. And that's okay, it's good and it's healthy. But we do not grieve without hope. We have that hope in Jesus Christ. And when it's all said and done, it will all be made right.

124

In Jesus Christ we have that hope that we will be together again with those whom we have lost, and we will be able to sit and swap stories and enjoy them once again. Amen.

Loved, Respected, Enjoyed
1ST Corinthians 13

August 8, 2018

Riley Young had an inimitable way to make friends - whoever he was with felt as if they were the most important person in the world. He had that remarkable ability to find something in common with everyone he met. And he communicated that commonality with warmth and sincerity.

My brother Paul and his wife were here to visit a year or so ago and joined us at Arby's for a meal after church. Paul and Riley sat next to each other and soon realized that they were in the U.S.M.C. reserves at the same time and talked at length about their similar experiences. I called Paul the other day to tell him Riley died and ask for prayers for Anne and their family. Paul was devastated. He said, "I was planning to come down and visit Riley soon." No mention of his brother or son to visit here. His intention was to come to see his new found friend Riley Young.

My own friendship with Riley began shortly after I first arrived here. We ended up walking down the hall together after the 11:00 a.m. worship service. We discovered quickly we had a lot in common - a love of Jesus Christ, certainly, a love of Fairfield Church, definitely but the true bond came when I apologized for stopping every few feet to turn off a light or turn down a thermostat. I said, "a penny saved is a penny given" and Riley replied, "we are going to get along just fine."

Riley had that way of being able to find something in common with everyone. He was a humble man who saw value in everyone he met. He never held himself out as better than anyone else. He could have. He was very, very successful - his academic achievements, his outstanding career with Verizon, his financial acumen, his ability to understand and work with numbers, by all worldly measures Riley was someone who rose well above the crowd with all of his skills and accomplishments.

Yet he remained humble. He was always willing to help anyone at any time whether it was financial advice, or greeting people coming into worship, setting up chairs and tables (no one ever asked him for handyman assistance though!). Selfless in giving - never seeking or wanting credit even on his deathbed his concern was for the wellbeing of his youngest grandchild.

His word was always true. Riley was our head usher for the month of December for all the years that I have been here. You don't know what a relief it has been for me to know that in the middle of all the other responsibilities that come along with Advent and Christmas, I never once had to think about the doors being open, people being greeted, bulletins handed out or any of the other jobs Riley handled without fanfare or notice. If he said he was going to do something, I counted it as done.

Riley's loyalty was second to none. Not just loyalty to responsibilities but loyalty to the people he loved. He loved Fairfield Church and all of its members and staff. It always brought him great joy to be a part of this church family. He was especially loyal to the Union Sunday School Class. He never missed a Sunday unless he and Anne were away with family. The receptions that the Union Class put on after a funeral of one of their members were always well done and Riley could always be counted to help set up and break down with his own style of precision. You could always count on Riley.

His friends and co-workers knew that he would always be willing to do anything to be of service to any of them. (It doesn't surprise me to look and see so many people who used to work with Riley at the phone company and so many whom he befriended over the years.) Riley enjoyed helping out anyone who needed. He probably was financial guide to many of you here today. He loved working with numbers and especially loved working with numbers to help people to become more financially secure in their lives. His advice whether financial or spiritual or otherwise was always sage and worth listening to. I know, in my ministry here, I could always ask Riley for his advice or opinion and he gave it freely and wisely. And I know I am just one among many who had that blessing.

Riley was a wonderful storyteller. The day he and my brother Paul sat at the table swapping stories of their Marine Corps days (Yes, I, like you, have a hard time imagining gentle Riley as a Marine but it is true). All of us around the table were spell bound as he would weave story after story of some incident or person he met or some humorous time. None of us wanted the lunch time to end. He had an eye for detail, which I am sure helped in his career, but which also made him a master storyteller. And often his stories had some moral lesson to teach or some greater point to make.

Riley always cared more about others than himself. He was a caring and compassionate man. In his final days on earth, he was more concerned about others who were ill or going through tough times. While any one of us in the same condition wouldn't even think of anyone but ourselves, Riley was giving instructions to Anne to make sure that this person and that person got handwritten notes to let them know that they were in his heart and prayers. He never thought more highly of himself than he did for others.

Riley was a gentle leader who valued nothing more in any group, whether work or church or family than to build consensus so that everyone might feel valued and important because in Riley's eyes they were just that. I am told and I believe it that Riley saw the value in and could deal with even the most difficult personality. He could see the good in everyone and he had a remarkable ability to bring that good out of them.

His compassion and deep love were most visible and the strongest in his love for his family. He adored Anne and cherished every moment of their 42 years together. His children and especially the grandchildren were the joy of his life. He loved each one a little more than the other. He would do anything at any time for any one of them or for all of them. His family was the center of his world and he loved them deeply and truly and unconditionally.

There is one phrase that sums up the life of Riley Young: he was a Christ-like man. You see the very cornerstone Riley's life was his faith in Jesus Christ and his desire to grow in that faith throughout his life. That indeed is what Riley did. The passage which we read earlier from I Corinthians 13 will always remind me of how Riley lived his life as a follower of Jesus Christ. He brought love to life. He had tremendous love in his heart for church and family and friends and co-workers, but he didn't let it rest quietly in his heart. He lived out that love through acts of kindness, generosity, sympathy and compassion. He saw that love without actions was empty and actions without love were useless.

That very faith is Jesus Christ was the capstone of his life and his death. Riley knew that because of Jesus' life, death and resurrection that there was nothing that could ever separate him from the love of God! Death was not something to be feared because it had been conquered 2000 years ago by Jesus Christ on that first Easter morning. That faith in Jesus Christ that guided Riley Young in his life is now his reality. What he once believed; he now sees face to face. I have no doubt in my mind that Jesus Christ welcomed Riley into the kingdom of Heaven with the greeting of "Well done, thou good and faithful servant!"

I don't want to deceive any of you, the pain we feel at the loss of Riley Young from our lives is real. It is hard to say goodbye to someone who was so special and who enriched our lives through the gift of his love for all of us. It is painful and we do grieve. But we grieve with hope. We know that as followers of Jesus Christ, we have that assurance that there will be that great reunion in the Kingdom of God. We know that because of the selfless gift of Jesus Christ we have the gift of eternal life through him. Yes, we are sad that we have lost Riley Young from our earthly lives, but we rejoice that he has gone ahead of us to that place where you never say "Goodbye" you only say "Hello".

Henri's Benediction

Words offered by Chaplain Steve Starzer at the committal service
for Assistant Chief Henri G. Moore, Jr. Hanover Fire/EMS

February 16, 2017

Hello everyone. For those of you who don't know me, I am Steve
Starzer one of the Chaplains for Hanover Fire/EMS. I am also
Henri's best friend. Okay, so actually I am Henri's best friend
number 2,768. I was honored and privileged to be able to spend a
good amount of time with Henri. When I first joined Hanover
Fire/EMS as a Chaplain, Henri took me under his wing and took me
around the County to every station where he introduced me to
everyone and his brother.

Spending a lot of time together in a car allowed us to have some
great conversations. We talked about everything under the sun from
past fire experiences to family. I tried to learn as much about this
Department as I could from Henri and peppered him with questions
about staffing, shifts, equipment, stations and procedures. He in turn
would ask me Biblical questions. He wanted me to explain the Book
of Revelation to him. I came out on the short of the stick on those
questions!

I remember we were riding together one day shortly after an
Academy Graduation. At that ceremony I offered the Benediction.
Those of you who have attended a ceremony where I offer the
benediction, you have learned that it is not a prayer but an expression
of one person's hope or desires for those whom he is addressing.
Henri was fascinated by that, so he asked me to say more about it.
So, I explained to him that a Benediction is an ancient tradition
particularly in the Judeo-Christian family. When two people are
parting from each other, generally the older one offers a blessing or
a wish for the other.

It is a very natural thing to do. We do it all the time. We tell our kids,
"be careful". We jokingly say to someone, "Stay out of trouble!"
When we know our time is limited with each other, we want to make
sure we say what is on our hearts.

One of the last conversations I had with Henri, he said, "Tell them to love each other." I think Henri knew this would be his Benediction to all of us: his family, his friends, and his uniformed brothers and sisters. His words were almost a direct quote from Jesus himself as he wrapped us His earthly pilgrimage. Jesus said, "Love one another. As I have loved you, so you must love one another."

Henri wasn't asking us to do anything he didn't already do for all of us. Henri had a tremendous capacity to love and it showed in every breathe he took. He loved his family. He was always bragging to me about how wonderful his family is and how his greatest joy was spending time with them. He loved his Lord and he loved his church family, his Pastor, his Sunday School class and all his brothers and sisters in Jesus Christ. And he most certainly loved the Brotherhood of those who shared his love of serving our communities through the Fire and Emergency Medical Services. You know Henri loved each and every one of us.

It shouldn't come as a surprise to any of us that his Benediction to each of us is that we should love one another. Henri left us a legacy of love. His love for us will always be a memory we cherish. But cherishing it is not enough. Can we take that legacy of love and put it into practice in our lives? Can we learn to love those God has placed around us in such a manner that the legacy we leave behind is measured not in dollars and cents but in the depth and the breadth of the love we have shared? That is how we honor Henri's life. That is how we write our own Benedictions.

A Sure Foundation

Wedding homily on the occasion of the marriage of
Robert Weyant & Lisa Bowdish

Matthew 7:24

October 5, 1996

> Jesus said, *"Therefore everyone who hears these words and puts them
> into practice is like a wise man who built his house on the rock. The
> rain came down, the streams rose and the winds blew against the house,
> yet it did not fall because it had its foundation on the rock. But
> everyone who hears these words of mine and does not put them into
> practice is like a foolish man who built his house on sand. The rain
> came down, the streams rose, the winds blew and beat against the house
> and it fell with a great crash. When Jesus had finished saying these
> things the crowds were amazed at this teaching because he taught as
> one who had authority and not as their teachers of the law."*

I know this text is not one we usually think about for weddings. We
are more familiar with passages such as First Corinthians 13 which
speaks to us of the topic of love. We think that weddings are only
about love. But I think that what intrigues me most about that
passage and why I feel it's so appropriate for a wedding is because
you two are entering into the business of building a home and how
you build that home will determine how that home lasts through all
the years of your life together. I'm not talking about literally building
a new house but what I am saying is that a wedding is the building
of a new life together - a home. So using this passage we can see the
importance of how it is that you build this new life together. The
fact is that into every marriage and into anyone's life comes times of
great turbulence. There will be all sorts of times in your lives where
there are struggles for each of you individually and struggles for both
of you together. It is in those times where how the foundation is
built in that home that the two of you build together will determine
how your marriage weathers those storms of this life. So I would
urge you and challenge you to build your foundation, the foundation
of your home together upon the rock of Jesus Christ, on his
teachings, on the way that he lived his life. Not just hearing the

words that Jesus spoke, but living the words that he spoke and if you can do that then the foundation of your marriage together will be a firm one, a sure one, one that will last through all the storms of this life and will grow stronger with each passing year.